BLACK&DECKER®

THE COMPLETE GUIDE TO

BACKYARD RECREATION
PROJECTS

- **Sports Courts & Outdoor Games**
- **Play Structures & Treehouses**
- **Outdoor Entertainment**

by Eric W. Smith

Creative Publishing international

MINNEAPOLIS, MINNESOTA
www.creativepub.com

Creative Publishing
international

Copyright © 2010
Creative Publishing international, Inc.
400 First Avenue North, Suite 300
Minneapolis, Minnesota 55401
1-800-328-0590
www.creativepub.com
All rights reserved

Printed in U.S.A. by R.R. Donnelly

10 9 8 7 6 5 4 3 2 1

Library of Congress Cataloging-in-Publication Data

The complete guide to backyard recreation projects : sports courts &
outdoor games, play structures & treehouses, outdoor entertainment.
      p. cm.
  Includes index.
  At head of title: Black & Decker.
  Summary: "More than 25 complete DIY projects to create play
spaces for family members of all ages"--Provided by publisher.
  ISBN-13: 978-1-58923-518-2 (soft cover)
  ISBN-10: 1-58923-518-5 (soft cover)
  1. Garden structures. 2. Recreation--Equipment and supplies. I.
Black & Decker Corporation (Towson, Md.) II. Title.

  TH4961.C6534 2010
  690'.89--dc22

2010002260

The Complete Guide to Backyard Recreation Projects
Created by: The Editors of Creative Publishing international, Inc., in cooperation with Black & Decker.
Black & Decker® is a trademark of The Black & Decker Corporation and is used under license.

President/CEO: Ken Fund

Home Improvement Group

Publisher: Bryan Trandem
Managing Editor: Tracy Stanley
Senior Editor: Mark Johanson
Editor: Jennifer Gehlhar

Creative Director: Michele Lanci-Altomare
Art Direction/Design: Jon Simpson, Brad Springer, James Kegley

Lead Photographer: Joel Schnell
Set Builder: James Parmeter
Production Managers: Linda Halls, Laura Hokkanen

Author: Eric W. Smith
Page Layout Artist: Danielle Smith
Technical Reviewer: John Drigot
Shop Help: Charles Boldt
Proofreader: Mary Ann Knox
Illustrator: George Barile

Contents

The Complete Guide to
Backyard Recreation Projects

Contents (Cont.)

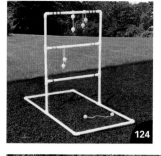

Contents (Cont.)

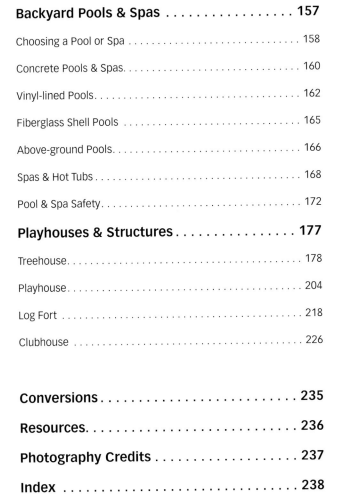

Introduction

The purpose of this book is to encourage recreation—to show you how to build play structures, set up game courts, create satisfying places to have fun and relax without having to drive to some far-away playground or amusement park. The book covers a wide range of backyard recreation projects, with ideas for all ages and interests—from sandboxes to porch swings, obstacle courses to outdoor kitchens, backyard putting greens to shuffleboard courts. Learn how to make an elaborate, two-story playset. See the best way to hang a tire swing. Find out the secret ingredient needed to make homemade water slides slippery, and what pickleball is all about. Find out how thick playground mulch needs to be to cushion a fall, where to safely locate a firepit, and how to create a fun and challenging obstacle course.

Discover the secret to building a treehouse without killing the tree, construct a mini half-pipe skateboard ramp, make your own glass-smooth backyard skating rink, install a zip line for fast, airborne rides, or set up your very own backyard drive-in theater to relax with friends. They're all here, along with dozens of other projects and ideas that will appeal to every member of your family. Most of the projects can be built within a few hours to a few days by homeowners with average construction skills. And all of the projects can be accomplished using everyday materials from local home centers.

The backyard is an important escape for everyone, not just kids. Although some of the projects in this book are intended for kids (which is not to say that adults can't play on them, too), the majority of the projects can be enjoyed by kids, teenagers, and adults alike.

With all of the electronic amusements available now it's sometimes hard to push the kids (and ourselves) off the couch and out the door. The projects in this book create reasons to get outside and be active, reminding us of the joys of whacking a ball, climbing high, jumping and running and yelling for no good reason—reminding us that having fun is important for all of us.

Safety ▸

A generation ago, nobody got too worked up about making everything child-safe. We just went out and played. And we all have the scars to prove it. Although accidents can never be entirely avoided, you should make every effort to reduce their frequency and severity. There is almost always a reason why accidents happen, and it's almost always preventable—a missing guard rail, an exposed sharp or pointy edge, nothing to cushion a fall, poor construction, or simply general inattentiveness. You can find more information about safety throughout this book, as well as by following links to safety organizations (see Resources, page 236).

Projects for Outdoor Recreation & Play

Just outside your back door you will find a whole world of enjoyment only a few steps away. With the pressures of work and school and the distracting glow of computers, game systems, and television, this outdoor world is sometimes neglected or even forgotten, but it's there, waiting.

The photos on the following pages show a few of the almost endless possibilities for recreation and fun that you can build in your backyard—possibilities that can transform the backyard from simply being that stretch of lawn you have to mow on weekends to a fun, relaxing spot that the whole family looks forward to enjoying. Use these photos as starting points and as sources for design ideas that you can incorporate into your own unique projects. Whether you're looking for a way for the kids to get exercise, a distraction for a restless teenager, or a new and more satisfying place for the adults to sit and relax, you'll find inspiration and ideas here.

A swing, a climbing wall and a slide are extra features that can add fun and originality to this expansive play structure.

Playground systems can be as small as a slide and fort. You can buy a complete package and have it assembled for you by professionals, or you can design and build your own, adding on to it or altering it in other ways as your kids grow.

Drive the metal stakes and fill the horseshoe pits surrounding them with sand to provide a landing area. Then start pitching.

Once you build a fort, it's simple to add on a swingset and other accessories. Often manufacturers will sell accessories that can be woven into your custom designs, too. Share your design with the dealer or manufacturer so they can advise on available additions.

A treehouse transforms a large tree into a secret world of adventure.

Seesaws are a timeless and simple form of playground entertainment. Attach sturdy boards to a pivot point, add handles, and you've made a seesaw.

A rope hanging from a tree branch can provide the support for a great swing.

Playhouses can be simple or elaborate; either can provide a secret hideaway and a special place for play.

Playsets with forts invite creativity and inspire imagination and flights of fancy. Be sure to talk to your children about appropriate safety precautions.

Turn your backyard into a water park using little more than a long sheet of plastic and a hose.

Tire swings are a great way to make recycling fun. Find a clean, worn-out tire (watch out for steel belting), a strong rope and a good tree, and you've got a swing that will last for years. Be sure to drill some drainage holes in the tire tread.

Monkey bars are simple, but any kid can find at least six games to play on them, plus variations. They are also excellent for building upper body strength and improving coordination.

A climbing wall has hand-holds and foot-holds attached to a vertical wooden surface. Short climbing walls are fun for most ages. Taller walls are great training for rock climbing, but they often require harnesses and other protective equipment.

A zip line is strung between two trees with just enough slack that a kid (or adult) can grab onto a trolley device and take a ride down the line. The sag in the cable and a stop several feet from the end safely stop the trolley.

Cold winters create new opportunities for backyard play. With 6-mil poly plywood, 2 × 6s, and a few thousand gallons of water, you can create a personal skating rink in your own backyard.

Put snow to good use as a building material for forts and caves. One fun exercise is to cut building blocks from settled snow and stack them into walls.

A simple wood sandbox is a perfect play area for young children. Make certain to police the sandbox regularly, and if it is positioned outdoors permanently, make a cover for it.

With an inexpensive basketball hoop and an open driveway you can recreate the excitement of the Final Four. Here a portable hoop is shown, but in this book we'll show you how to install a classic built-in or wall-mounted version.

A backyard spa makes a perfect place to unwind. Add some privacy screening if sightlines are an issue and the spa is transformed into a romantic destination.

The backyard grill can be taken to new extremes when a fully-functioning kitchen is installed on your patio or three-season porch. A set-up with actual kitchen appliances and fixtures will require a roof structure.

Enjoy the warmth of an outdoor fire even in a smaller yard with a backyard firepit.

Outdoor theaters bring a whole new meaning to "outdoor living." It may seem like an expensive luxury, but with a DVD player, an LCD projector, a sound system, and a screen, you can create an outdoor theater with ease in your own backyard.

The benefits of a backyard swimming pool are immediately apparent, but be aware of the costs and the upkeep requirements before you commit.

A putting green can be constructed in your yard using real turf or by using artificial turf or even a putting green kit. They are big fun and help sharpen your golf skills.

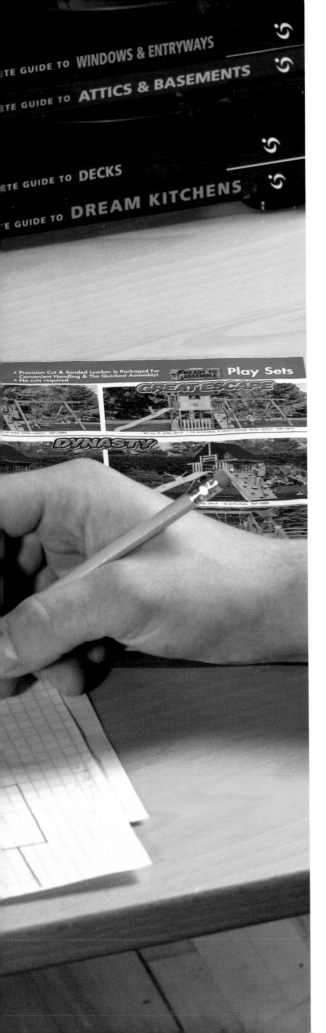

Planning & Basics

Before starting a large project, it's important to get a clear idea of where to build it, what landscaping work is involved, and how much it will cost. If the structure will be anywhere close to the property lines and will be difficult to move after you build it, make sure you know exactly what setbacks are required in your area. Talk to an inspector about what you're planning to do—it doesn't cost anything; in fact, you probably will get some good advice or handouts about construction details, and it might save you from big problems later on.

If you live in an area with a neighborhood homeowner's association, or your house is part of a condominium development, check your deed and talk to your neighbors before starting any permanent or semi-permanent projects to find out if there are restrictions. You'll also need to know how deep to dig footings and what to do if you have bad soil or a high water table. This all sounds worse than it is—one or two phone calls usually resolve all of these questions, and it's best to get the answers at the start.

You also should estimate the cost of materials to avoid surprises. For complicated projects like a shed or a large play area, lumberyards and home centers will estimate costs for you if you give them a detailed scale drawing of what you plan to build. It's always a good idea to add 10% for waste and mistakes. One of the first rules of construction is that no matter what you're building, it will take twice as long and cost twice as much as you thought it would.

In this chapter:

- Working & Building Safely
- Finding the Right Spot
- Outdoor Building Materials
- Tools

Working & Building Safely

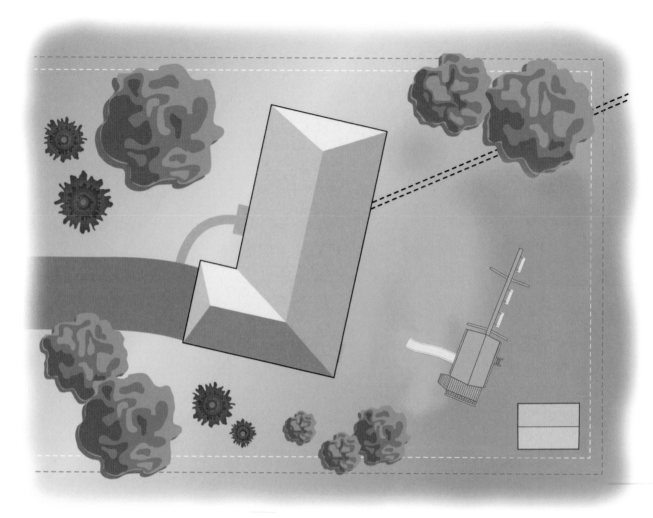

Before building anything, locate your lot lines and any buried utilities. Make note of overhead utility lines, and make sure your play structure is far enough away from them so the two don't touch—the general recommendation is to make sure utility lines are at least twice the height of the structure (which includes most building projects, including swingsets). Play areas must be at least six feet from any building, tree, or other obstacle. The clear area in front and back of swings must be at least twice the height of the swingset (measured from the center of the swingset).

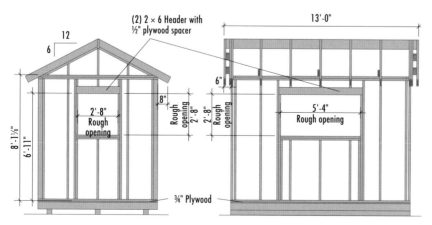

Before buying any lumber, make scaled construction drawings on graph paper. It will make buying materials and building the structure much easier and help you avoid expensive mistakes. If you need to obtain a building permit, inspectors will also want to see your construction drawings.

Safety Equipment

Protective gloves play two important roles when you are working outdoors: they protect your hands from abrasions when working with tools or handling building and landscaping materials, and they prevent contact with chemicals such as solvent-based finishing products. Wear well-fitted work gloves whenever they do not interfere with important dexterity concerns. Wear rubber gloves when working with solvent-base paints, stains, and sealers or other chemicals that are not suitable for skin contact.

Protective eyewear is perhaps the most important safety gear you can wear. Quality protective eyewear has lightweight, shatterproof lenses that are resistant to fogging. Some are tinted to protect against UV rays. If you will be working around chemicals or airborne irritants, wear safety goggles that fit your face snugly. Some prescription glasses are rated as safety glasses, but don't assume that yours are: wear goggles over them if you are not certain.

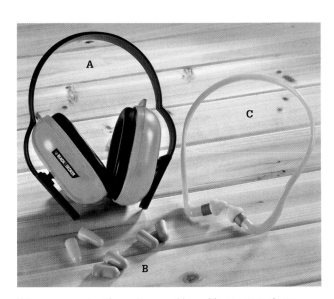

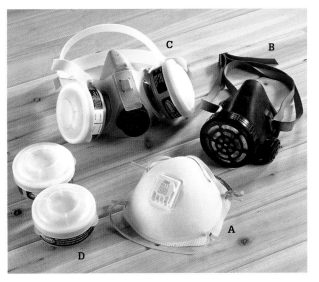

Wear ear protection when working with power tools or working around other loud noises. Basic construction earmuffs (A) are inexpensive and reliable. For a slightly higher cost you can purchase electronic versions that feature noise canceling so only objectionable and dangerous noises are blocked. Disposable foam ear plugs (B) will do in a pinch, but they tend to loosen. Foam earplugs connected with a head band (C) stay put longer.

Respiratory protection is worn in areas where ventilation is poor or whenever you are cutting treated lumber or working around airborne particulates, noxious gases or fumes. A paper mask with an N-95 rating and two straps (A) will block particulates such as sawdust, insulation dust, and most allergens. A half mask (B) has replaceable filters that block out additional particles, along with some fumes. A respirator (C) provides the most complete breathing protection. It has interchangeable cartridges (D).

Finding the Right Spot

After you decide on a project for your yard—but before you buy any supplies—you'll need to figure out exactly how big the project needs to be and then lay it out on the yard to make sure it's going to fit. If you're constructing a large play structure or sports court, draw an accurate site plan of your yard on a sheet of graph paper. If you need a permit, the building department will also require copies. Draw in the property lines, existing structures, trees, gardens, and any other nearby features that may impact your new project. Make sure to note the location and height of overhead utility lines. They should be distant at least twice the height of the swingset or fort; if not, contact an electrician or the utility company about having the utility lines moved or raised.

Make several copies of the site plan, then sketch in the structure you plan to build so you can determine if you have enough clearance, both for the structure and for the activity that will be going on around it. Playgrounds need an additional six feet of clearance all the way around the built structure and swingsets have to have clear space from their center equal to twice their height (thus, if the swingset is eight feet high, you'll need 16 feet of open space on both sides of the beam).

The Yard Survey ▶

Accurate yard measurements are critical for planning the size and placement of backyard structures. They also help you work out how to level uneven areas, drain wet spots, and landscape. To sketch your survey, follow these steps:

Sketch your yard and all its main features on a sheet of paper. Assign a key letter to each point. Measure all straight lines and record the measurements on a notepad.

Take triangulated measurements to locate other features, such as trees that don't lie along straight lines. Triangulation involves locating a feature by measuring its distance from any two points whose positions are known.

Plot irregular boundaries and curves, and note high spots or low-lying areas that need attention. Plot these features by taking a series of perpendicular measurements from a straight reference line, such as the edge of your house or garage.

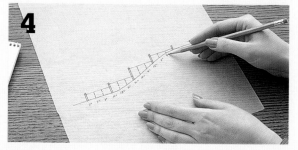

Sketch elevations to show slopes. Measure the vertical drop of a slope using different-sized stakes and string. Connect the string to the stakes so it is perfectly horizontal. Measure the distance between the string and ground at 2-ft. intervals along the string.

Improving Uneven Ground

Create level areas for playing lawn sports such as croquet, badminton, and bocce. Drive stakes to outline the perimeter of the area you want to level. Run mason's strings between the stakes and level them. Find the high point and add soil to raise the surrounding ground. Or, find the low point and excavate around it.

Use a hand tamp to compact the soil you add. Don't overtamp the soil where you'll be planting grass or it could become too dense for a healthy lawn.

How to Improve Drainage

Runoff channel

Remove a section of sod and dig a shallow drainage trench sloping to the center, creating a V shape. Use the shovel to smooth the sides as you work.

Replace the sod in the trench, compressing it against the soil and then thoroughly watering it to create a natural-looking swale.

Terrace Hillsides with Retaining Walls

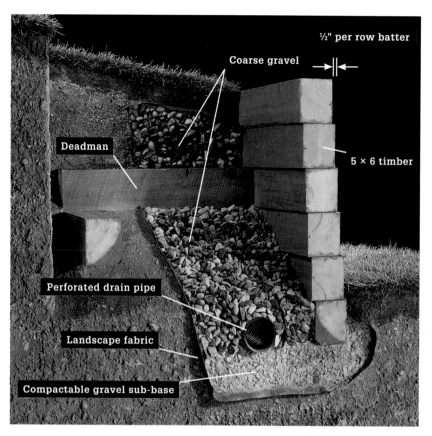

½" per row batter

Coarse gravel

5 × 6 timber

Deadman

Perforated drain pipe

Landscape fabric

Compactable gravel sub-base

Timbers are a fast, relatively inexpensive way to build a retaining wall. Fill the space behind them with gravel to keep them dry, and lock the wall against the hillside with T-shaped "deadman" anchors.

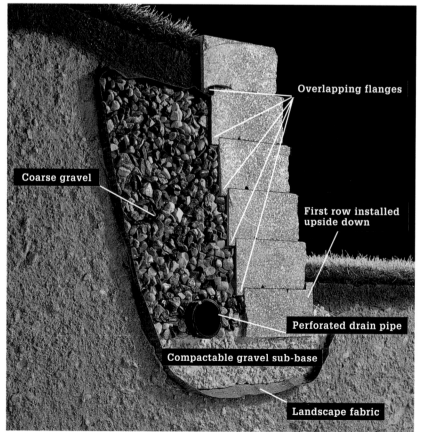

Overlapping flanges

Coarse gravel

First row installed upside down

Perforated drain pipe

Compactable gravel sub-base

Landscape fabric

Interlocking blocks are a permanent solution to a sloping yard. They don't require mortar and are simple to install.

Why Terrace? ▸

Using retaining walls to create terraces in your yard is an effective way to make sloping ground usable for recreational activities.

Safe Surfaces ▶

One of the keys to a safe playground is having a surface that cushions your children when they fall. Falls account for approximately three-quarters of all playground injuries, according to the U.S. Consumer Products Safety Commission. Including a safe surface, therefore, is an important part of your play area.

Stay away from hard surfaces such as asphalt, concrete, dirt, and grass. Some of the more common loose-fill materials you can use for your playground include:

Wood mulch: Wood mulch is essentially wood that has been chopped into small pieces by a wood chipper. It is available by the truckload or can be purchased by the bag.

Wood chips: Wood chips are small pieces of wood, twigs and leaves of similar sizes that have been through a wood chipper. The chips come from tree limbs, branches, and brush. It is also readily available.

Engineered wood fibers: This material is uniformly-sized shredded hardwood fibers.

Sand: Both fine sand and coarse sand can be used for playground surfaces. Sand is fairly inexpensive; however, it's easily displaced and gets in children's clothing.

Pea gravel: Pea gravel is small round pieces of washed gravel, generally less than ⅜" in diameter. Gravel is less likely to attract animals than sand or wood. The disadvantage is that gravel can freeze together and become hard in freezing temperatures.

Shredded tires: Shredded tires are just that: shredded tires. They have superior shock-absorbing qualities and will not deteriorate over time. Be sure to use shredded tires that do not contain wire from steel-belted tires and that have been treated to keep them from discoloring clothing.

Each of these surfaces is relatively easy to install in a play area. Apply the material you choose to a depth of 12 inches and extend it at least 70 inches in all directions from the play equipment for maximum protection against falls. For swings, the surface should extend to a distance twice the height of the swings both in front and in back of each swing. If you have an eight-foot swing, for instance, cushion a surface that extends 16 feet in front and in back of the swing.

You'll either need to build a retaining barrier or dig a pit to contain the surface material. The area should have good drainage so the material doesn't sit in water. Most surfaces need periodic maintenance, such as grading or adding more material to keep an adequate depth.

Wood mulch

Wood chips

Engineered wood fibers

Sand

Pea gravel

Shredded tires

Outdoor Building Materials

Backyard recreational structures have to stand up to years of hard use and hard weather, and any material used to make them must be both sturdy and rot- or rust-resistant.

Generally, the least expensive and most widely available wood used for exterior structures is pressure-treated pine (here, "pine" typically includes several evergreen species related to pine, including spruce and fir). Current treatment solutions for preserving wood include C-A (Copper Azole), ACQ (Alkaline Copper Quartenary), and Borate. All may be used for any backyard application as long as the wood will not be exposed to saltwater on a regular basis. If your wood is green-treated (C-A or ACQ), you must use hot-dipped, galvanized fasteners that are made of triple-dipped, stainless steel, or specially coated screws approved for treated wood. Green-treated wood products cause metal to corrode rapidly, which can lead to premature structural failure if you use unapproved metal hardware. CCA, the controversial arsenic-based treatment chemical, was pulled from the market several years ago.

Cedar, which is naturally rot-resistant, is sold at most lumberyards and home centers, though in some areas it may be available only through special order. Although cedar generally costs more than treated pine, it will not last as long as treated lumber if it's in contact with the ground (you can increase cedar's rot resistance by treating it with wood preservative). Often, builders will use treated pine to construct structural members such as posts and framing, and then use cedar, which is warmer and more attractive, for decking, railings, and trim.

Other naturally rot-resistant woods sometimes sold at lumberyards are redwood, cypress, and ipé (a South American wood) but these are not as widely available and can be prohibitively expensive.

Composite and plastic lumber suitable for exterior projects are sold in increasing quantities and selections at home centers and lumberyards. It's more expensive than treated wood, but has a perfectly smooth appearance and won't warp, crack, or splinter as they age. It's an excellent choice for trim and decking, but it is not rated for structural use. Decking must be supported every 16 inches to avoid sagging. This type of lumber can be cut and drilled just like wood but may require different fasteners, so check the instructions when you buy it.

Cedar and pressure-treated pine are used frequently for building recreational structures, but composite boards and other species of wood can be used effectively under some conditions. Wood and wood-based products for outdoor building include: Douglas fir (A), cedar (B), pressure-treated pine (C), hollow composite material (D), solid composite material (E).

Use exterior-rated fasteners for outdoor projects. Shown here is a sampling of outdoor fasteners and hardware: Triple-dipped galvanized joist hangers (A); galvanized/exterior-rated carriage bolts, lag bolts, washers and nuts (B); triple-dipped galvanized post standoffs (C); galvanized corner brackets (D); joist-hanger nails (E); coated deck screws in various lengths (F); galvanized common nails (G).

Hauling Materials ▸

You can save delivery charges (usually $35 to $50) and control delivery times by hauling landscape materials yourself in a pickup or trailer. The yard workers at the supply center will load your vehicle free of charge with a front-end loader or skid loader. Do not overload your vehicle. Although most operators are aware of load limits, they will typically put in as much as you tell them to. As a general rule of thumb, a compact truck (roughly the size of a Ford Ranger) can handle one scoop of dirt, sand or gravel, which is about ¾ of a cubic yard; a half-ton truck (Ford F-150) will take a scoop and a half (a little over a cubic yard), and a three-quarter ton truck (F-250) can haul two scoops (one and a half cubic yards) safely. Be sure to check the gross vehicle weight and payload data label on the driver's door.

Tools

Most of the projects in this book can be built with standard construction and yard tools, but you may want to rent specialty tools on a project-by-project basis. Everything from small hand tools and power tools to front-end loaders are available at tool rental stores, and it's well worth a visit or a look at a rental catalog to see what's available. Although rentals can be expensive, they can literally save days of hard labor, not to mention sore backs.

Power tools that will be useful for your outdoor building project include: 360° laser level on stand (A), plunge router (B), circular saw (C), power miter saw (D), cordless pneumatic nailer (E), drill/driver (F), jigsaw (G), cordless impact driver (H), random-orbital sander (I), belt sander (J), drill bits and counterbores (K).

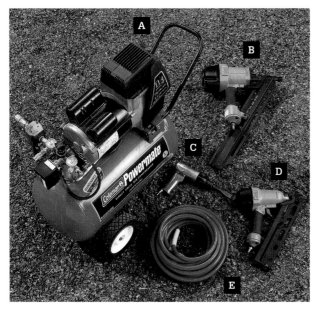

Pneumatic tools include: air compressor (A), framing-nail gun (B), air hammer with chisel bits (C), finish-nail gun (D), air hose (E).

Specialty tools include: tamping machines (A), sod cutter (B), power auger (C), hand tamper (D), chain saw (E).

A two-person power auger makes quick work of posthole digging. Be sure to have your property inspected and flagged for underground lines before you dig.

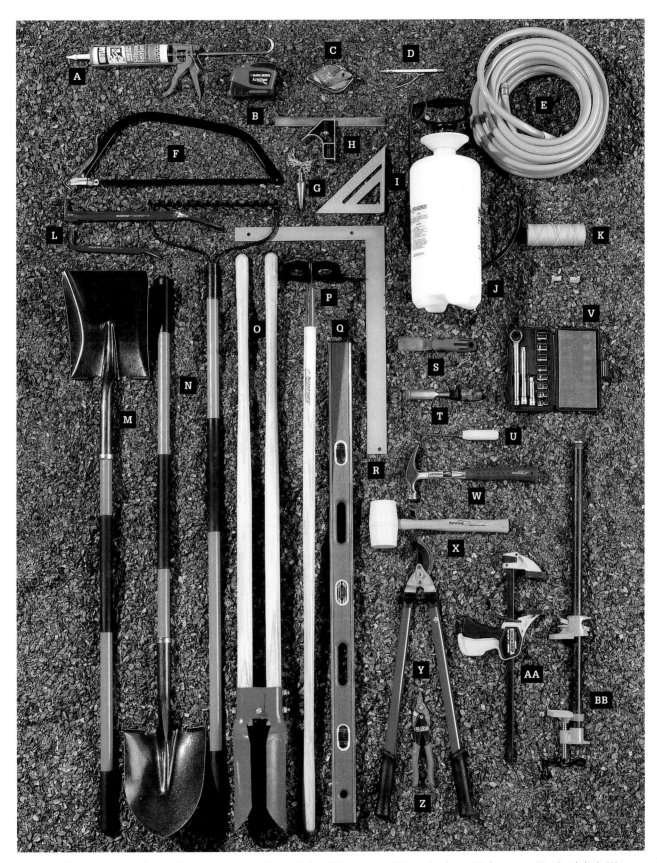

Hand tools include: caulk gun (A), tape measure (B), chalk line (C), compass (D), garden hose (E), bow saw (F), plumb bob (G), combination square (H), speed square (I), pressure sprayer (J), mason's line (K), pry bars (L), square and round shovels (M), garden rake (N), posthole digger (O), hoe (P), carpenter's level (Q), framing square (R), putty knife (S), wood chisel (T), awl (U), socket wrench (V), hammer (W), rubber mallet (X), pruning shears (Y), metal shears (Z), bar clamps (AA), pipe clamps (BB).

Play Structures

Kids love playgrounds. A playground is one of the dwindling places kids are allowed to run wild without heavy supervision or disapproving looks. It is a sanctuary where a child can create rich and exciting alternative worlds, from just a slide and swing and wood tower. A playground is also a great place to get exercise.

Playgrounds do not need to be elaborate and expensive to be fun, but they do need to be carefully designed and maintained for safety. Kids love to climb and jump and swing and explore: If you can create a place where they can play and you won't worry, everyone wins.

A good design for a two-year-old is very different from one built for an eight-year-old. Commercial play areas try to offer a blend of activities—low platforms, crawling tunnels, and sandboxes for small children, combined with climbing ropes, monkey bars, large slides, and similarly challenging activities for older children. Another approach if you have young children is to start small and then build upward as the children get older.

In this chapter we'll feature some of the most popular options available for residential play structures. Then, we'll walk you through the process of building two of them—the first is an off-the-shelf, precut playground from a home center, and the second is a do-it-yourself playground built from standard size lumber and hardware. You can follow the instructions and build one of your own, or just use them as inspiration for your own design.

In this chapter:

- Choosing a Play System
- Playground Safety
- Precut Playground Kit
- DIY Playset
- DIY Swingset

Choosing a Play System

There are four basic routes to get a playground erected in your backyard. Not surprisingly, the more money you're willing to pay, the less work you'll have to do yourself. The simplest way to get a new backyard playground is to order one from a local company that specializes in building them. However, if you're handy and have basic tools, you can save a lot of money by buying a precut package and assembling it yourself. You can save even more by buying detailed plans and buying your own lumber and fasteners—or simply by doing it all yourself. Here's a basic overview of the options.

Hire a playground company. This is the simplest option. A number of local and national companies offer a wide range of models, from basic play areas to small mansions, that they will build and install. The advantage of hiring one of these companies is that they have experience, use high-quality materials, offer dozens of fun options, are up-to-date on all the codes and safety features, guarantee their work, and they don't require anything from you except money. The disadvantage is that it can be a lot of money—three to four times as much as a comparable precut package that you assemble yourself.

Buy a precut package. This option is the simplest and most failsafe for the DIYer. The playground is already designed, all the pieces are cut (although some packages require you to buy additional standard lengths of lumber), and all accessories and hardware are included. You'll have to dig holes and do some drilling and bolting, but other than that you just follow the instructions. Most companies offer a number of options and add-ons, so you can usually get everything you and your children want in a playground. Plus, the safety features are all designed in. The disadvantage is that you're paying several times the cost of the materials for someone to design the playground and cut and package all the pieces for you.

A playset structure is the heart of any backyard playground. Choosing the model you want is the first step toward deciding how much of the work, if any, you can handle by yourself.

Buy a plan. For anywhere from free to several hundred dollars you can buy (or download) detailed plans and lumber lists for a wide variety of playgrounds. The more expensive plans often include some hardware and accessories and may even offer customer support; the free plans are of widely varying quality, ranging from up-to-date plans available from lumberyards to reproductions of ancient magazine and book plans. These can be a good starting point for a moderately experienced DIYer who can read blueprints and make adjustments, as necessary.

Design and build your own. If you're an experienced builder and can make scaled drawings, this is the most economical way to go. However, this option will take more time than any of the other options—and this may be just what you're looking for: a fun project for your kids that is a fun project for you to build! With the availability of photos, plans, and how-to information on the Internet, it's not difficult to reverse-engineer features you're not sure about, and accessories like swings and slides always include installation guidelines. **Before building, make sure you have up-to-date information about safety features and requirements (see Consumer Product Safety Commission guidelines in the Resources section, page 236).**

Taking a DIY approach to design is a fine idea, but wherever possible try to rely on purchased components for critical components and structural parts, including climbing accessories, slides, swings and hardware.

Playground Safety

Safety is paramount to enjoying your backyard playground. And safety starts in the basic planning stage. For example, if you plan to build multiple play structures, keep at least nine feet of space between them. Securely mount the structures or anchor them to the ground and always follow manufacturer instructions.

In addition to planning your playground project wisely, you can make your play area safer by observing some basic rules when building it.

- Drive nailheads and set screwheads completely into the wood so the heads are flush with the surfaces. Nails or screws that stick out of the wood can pose a serious risk to children. When you've finished building your project, examine it for fasteners that are popping out. Also check for nails or screws that have gone completely through

boards and are sticking out the other side. If that happens, clip the end off or grind it down flush with the board.

- Countersink or counterbore holes for anchor bolts so the heads and nuts are recessed.
- Crimp hooks with pliers so sharp edges are not exposed.
- Conduct regular inspections of the structures and look for unusual wear and tear, loose boards or connections, and loose rails. Replace hardware if needed, only with identical hardware.

Playground Safety ▸

For more in-depth information on playground safety, visit the following websites:

- National Program for Playground Safety: uni.edu/playground
- US Consumer Product Safety Commission: cpsc.gov

Attention to safety details along with a thick cushion of soft mulch around the entire play area ensures that all the landings will be happy ones.

Are Post Footings Necessary? ▸

Pouring concrete footings to anchor structural components results in a rock-solid playground, but the process adds hard work and expense. Poured footings are not always necessary, especially if you're building a wide or low structure or using angled supports (like those used for swingsets). Here's a breakdown of the advantages and disadvantages of pouring concrete post footings:

ADVANTAGES
- Creates a stable, permanent base that won't tip or move or sag

- Anchors swingsets and other play equipment solidly
- Makes building on uneven ground easier
- Allows you to make tall, narrow structures and cantilevers without danger of tipping or movement
- Structure can eventually be converted to a storage or garden shed

DISADVANTAGES
- Adds time and expense to the project, especially if you are building in rocky or hard clay soil
- Structures that can't be moved or disassembled easily may interfere with future landscaping

Securing Playground Equipment

Add a wide, stable base to playground structure supports. Stabilize the base as much as possible by angling the supporting posts and adding crosspieces. Add additional stability by driving and fastening anchor stakes next to the base.

Screw-in anchors help keep playground structures from rocking or tipping, though they can be difficult to install in hard clay or rocky soil. Make sure anchors don't create a tripping hazard.

Spread the Playground Mulch ▸

According to the Consumer Product Safety Commission, about 40,000 children a year visit hospital emergency rooms due to falls from playground equipment. A safe playground will have a cushioning surface, such as mulch or wood chips. Most home playgrounds, however, are located directly on grassy lawns because that is an easy, cost-free surface. However, any grass lawn will become compacted and hard eventually, making falls dangerous. And, of course, you should never build a playground on hard surfaces like concrete or asphalt.

The supports for playground structures need to be anchored on solid, undisturbed ground, so the mulch layer is usually added after the playground is constructed. Once all of the structural elements are anchored, remove some dirt from around the play area—slightly slope the grade away from the supports for the tower and swings. The mulch should extend at least six feet out from all structures and 16 feet beyond the support

beam of a swing. The cushion layer should be installed over landscape fabric to a depth of at least 12 inches. You can reach that depth either by excavating or by adding landscape timbers around the edges to contain the mulch.

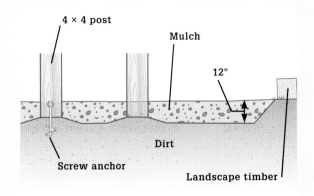

Precut Playground Kit

If you want to design and build a backyard playground that meets your needs, but you don't want to start from scratch, a good option is to buy a precut playground kit. Most home centers and a number of Internet suppliers sell do-it-yourself playground packages containing parts and hardware to make a complete play area. Some of the kits include all of the wood, while others include a list of lumber that you must buy with the set. Dozens of different designs are available, from a basic swingset and slide to elaborate, multilevel play areas with numerous extra features. Most manufacturers design their systems so that optional features can be easily added on.

Most playground systems are designed to be installed with poured concrete footings, but in some cases you may be able to get by with simply anchoring the posts (see page 37). If you choose not to pour

footings, it's even more important for the ground underneath the tower and swingset to be very level. To level and smooth the playground area and to stop grass and weeds from growing through it, cut out the sod in the play area, or at least in the area where the structures go, before you begin building.

Some playground kits include all the necessary drill bits and drivers. If your kit doesn't, you'll need a standard selection of spade bits and drill bits, as well as countersink bits for #6 and #8 screws. You'll also need a magnetized Phillips head driver for your drill.

Note: The instructions in the following project are intended as a general guide for installing a playground kit that includes precut lumber. The type of playground you purchase may use different materials and techniques than shown here.

Precut playground packages contain everything you need except tools. A homeowner with basic skills can put together a play area like this in one or two weekends.

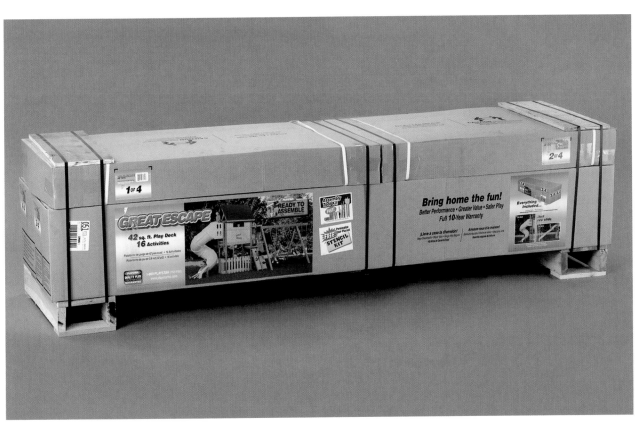

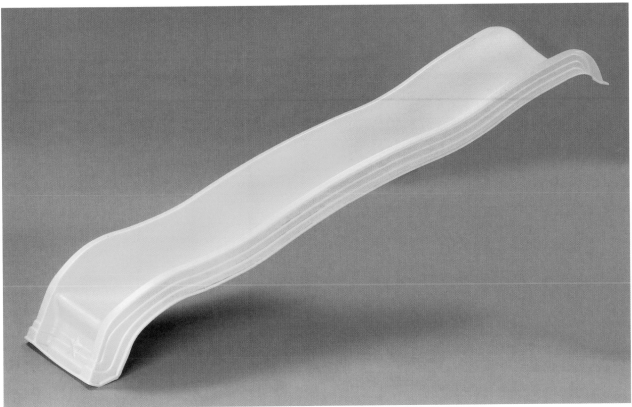

Playground kits generally contain all necessary hardware and accessories, and some or all of the wood (top photo). Additional accessories, such as slides, are purchased separately (bottom photo). If you need to purchase additional wood, the kit's shipping carton will show a list of extra lumber required (this will be an extra cost). Playground mulch must also be purchased separately. See page 27 for information about playground mulch.

Playground Kit

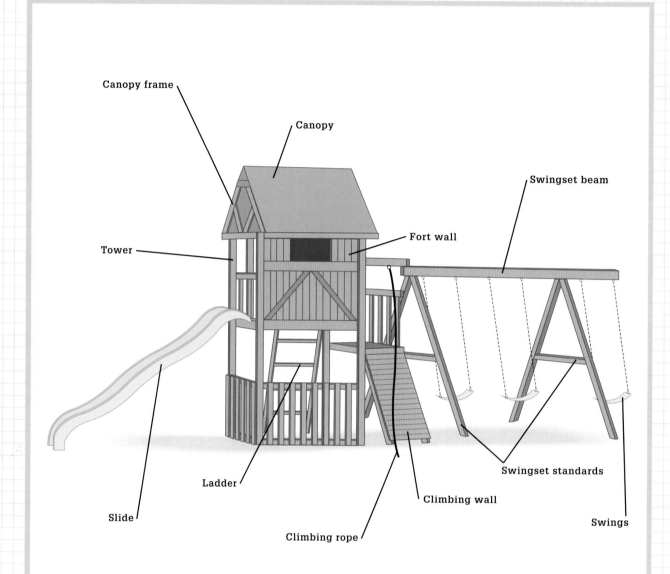

Canopy frame

Canopy

Swingset beam

Tower

Fort wall

Slide

Ladder

Climbing rope

Climbing wall

Swingset standards

Swings

Tools & Materials

Framing square
Carpenter's level
Socket wrench
Adjustable wrench
Drill/driver
Sawhorses
Shovels
Posthole digger
   (if screw-in anchors don't
   work with your soil)
Stakes

Mason's string
Line level
Power saw
Clamps
Ladder
Spacers
Screwdriver
Lag screws
Anchor screws
Playset kit
Eye and ear protection

Work gloves
2 × 6 or 2 × 8
Brackets
Bolts
1½", 2½" deck screws
Tape measure
Swing hangers
1½" panhead screws
Landscape fabric
Mulch
Screw-in anchors

How to Install a Playground Kit

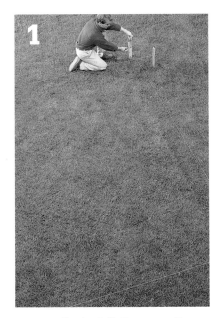

Prepare the installation area. Use strings and stakes to outline the area and then cut out the sod in the play area (buy or rent a sod cutter if you wish to replant the sod elsewhere in your yard). Level the ground. Where possible, level the ground using the lowest spot as a starting point and excavating high areas to that point. Add landscape fabric.

Begin assembling a tower. Towers are the principal structural elements in any playground kit. They support slides and other accessories. Generally, they are comprised of fairly simple frames and beams. For the kit shown here, assemble the framework of the tower one side at a time, and then join the sides together on top of flat pieces of 2 × 6 or 2 × 8. Use the drilling template included in the kit as a guide for driving countersunk screws. Locate screws carefully—metal brackets that cover the screwheads are often added later, so the screws have to be positioned carefully. Raise the tower.

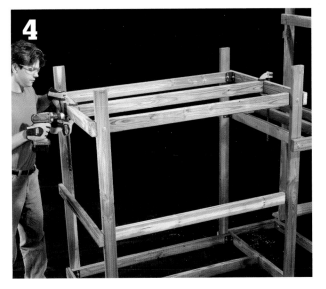

Screw the brackets to the tower frame corners, making sure that the bolt hole on the long side of the bracket lines up with the centers of the 2 × 4s behind it. Using the large holes in the brackets as guides, drill holes for the bolts. To avoid splintering the back sides, stop drilling as soon as the bit starts to poke through the back, then finish drilling from the other side. Check to make sure everything is still square, and then install and tighten the bolts.

Install the center joists that connect the platform frames, fastening them with countersunk 2½" deck screws. Make certain all screwheads are fully seated beneath the wood surface,

(continued)

5

Install the deckboards with 1½" deck screws driven into countersunk pilot holes, starting with the 2 outside pieces. Try to make sure the ends of the deck boards are aligned during installation—clamping a stop block or spacer block to the deck-board support will help align your workpieces. The drainage gaps between the deck boards must be less than ¼".

6

Extend the tower walls to the full height with additional 2 × 4 pieces. Use the drill guide or template (if provided with your kit) to ensure regular alignment of all screws.

7

Install the outer framework of 2 × 4s to support the roof of the playground structure, using corner brackets provided by the kit manufacturer.

8

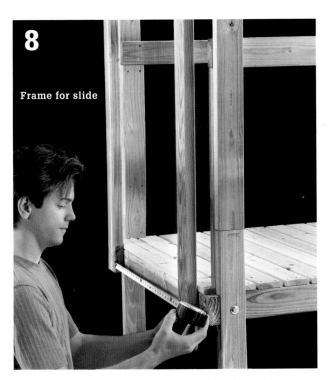

Frame for slide

Add additional framing to strengthen the sides of the tower. The framing on the right will help support the swingset and the climbing bar and climbing wall; the 2 × 4s on the left are used to support the slide.

9

Spacer

Install the bottom railings and the top back and side railings for the tower structure. Clamp a straight piece of wood on top of (or underneath) the railing at the 1" point to create the setback and to make installation easier. Cut spacers to make the gap even, but check the gap before screwing in the last few boards, just in case, and adjust if necessary.

10

Attach railings, siding, and trim. Install the front railing first, using a ³⁄₁₆" spacer. Then, add the trim pieces. This step is easier if you tilt the structure backwards to the ground—but don't try this without a helper.

11

Install the rest of the roof frame. Use clamps to hold pieces in position before attaching them. Check the center vertical pieces with a carpenter's level to make sure they are plumb.

(continued)

12

Begin building the swingset. The swing structure shown here is supported by a pair of angled posts in an A-frame configuration on the end farther from the tower, and a single angled leg on the tower end. Fasten the 3 legs of the swingset together (they are made with doubled 2 × 4s), and then bolt on the triangular bracket for each leg. Construct the assembly by bolting the triangular brackets together and then screwing on the crosspiece. Add the small brackets to the inside of the crosspiece, with the short legs against the crosspiece (inset). Trim the leg bottoms so they will lie flat on the ground.

13

Join the beams and legs. Screw the 2 × 6 beam pieces to the brackets, making sure the legs are exactly parallel and square to the beam. Drill the ⅜" holes for the bolts using the brackets as a guide. Then screw the second layer of 2 × 6s to the first with 2½" screws.

14

Swing hanger

Attach the swing hardware. First, turn the swing assembly over and place it on sawhorses. Drill guide holes and fasten the sides together with bolts. Drill guide holes for the swing hangers and lag screws and install them so that the moving hanger swings perpendicular to the beam.

15

Add the swingset to the tower. Lift the swingset into place and fasten it to the tower with a bolt through the swing beam and a 2 × 4 crosspiece near the base fastened with metal angles and bolts.

16

Installing the climbing wall. Attach the climbing wall supports to the tower frame with the provided brackets. The ends of the supports are angle-cut at the top and the bottom. Attach the top and bottom crossboards to the outer supports and then center the middle support board and attach it by driving deck screws through the crossboards and into the support.

17

Add the remaining crossboards in the climbing wall, working down from the top and making sure the boards are fitted tightly together.

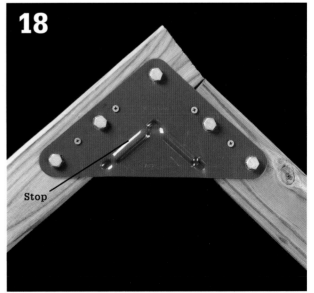

18

Stop

Start building the climbing bar assembly. The climbing bars function as a ladder that is mounted to the tower on the side opposite from the climbing wall. Assemble the climbing bar standards with four triangular metal brackets included with the kit. The stops on the sides of the brackets that contact the standard will set the correct angle for the standards if the boards are tight against the stops.

(continued)

Attach the climbing bars to the standards, making sure the standards are parallel and oriented correctly. Use 1¼" panhead screws to attach the bars at 12" intervals on the bottom leg and at 10¾" intervals along the top (or as directed by the instructions for your kit).

Connect the climbing bar to the tower. First, dig holes into the play surface at the correct locations for the legs of the climbing bar standards. Set the legs into the 2"-deep holes (inset), and then fasten the top ends of the standards to the tower with brackets and lag screws.

Anchor all sides of the swingset, along with the climbing bar and climbing wall, using screw-in anchors (see page 48). If the anchors don't work properly in your soil type, dig a 2-ft.-deep posthole, fill it with concrete, and set the anchor in that. Bolt the anchor to the structure with ⅜ × 1½" lag screws.

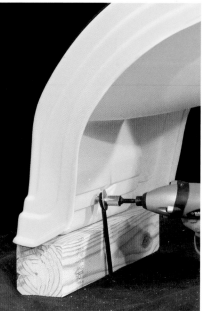

22

Attach the slide. First, position the slide (left photo) and then attach it to the tower at the top with fasteners as provided (or recommended) by the manufacturer. Then, bolt the slide at the base to a screw-in anchor. *Tip: Attach the bottom of the slide to a 4 × 4 spacer and then attach the spacer to a screw-in anchor (right photo). This provides a solid footing for the slide while raising it so the bottom is not completely covered by groundcover or mulch.*

23

Add other accessories, including swings, the roof, and the climbing rope. You'll need to drill access holes for the climbing rope in the climbing wall. Add approved groundcover (see page 27).

DIY Playset

If you want a playset, designing and building your own from scratch is not as easy or fast as buying a precut system, but if you have the tools and know-how you can save money and create a more unique and imaginative playset by doing it yourself.

The simplest way to get started is to design and build the playground in separate parts, beginning with a simple, rectangular platform. You can then add slides, a swingset, a climbing rope, and other features as your time and budget allow. Before you start, mark the area where the play structure will go in your yard, then add additional area for playground mulch (at least six feet out in all directions). Cut away the sod in this area and level the ground—preferably by digging out soil instead of filling in, since fill will continue to compress even after it is compacted.

Playset Hardware ▸

Although it's a little more work initially, the best way to make sure your playground will be solid and stable is to pour concrete footings and anchor the platform posts to the footings. Ideally, the footings should extend below the frostline (check with your local building department if you do not know your frostline depth). If you pour concrete footings, make sure that the concrete is covered by several inches of dirt or playground mulch to prevent injuries.

When building your playset, you can set the posts into postholes, add a few inches of gravel, and then fill the hole with concrete, or you can set the posts into exterior-rated metal post bases that are anchored to the concrete.

Note: Metal post bases are designed to work in groups and are not a good choice for single posts or even post pairs. They do not provide sufficient side-to-side rigidity.

If your structure is very wide or low to the ground, you can forego footings and instead bolt the posts to a framework of 2 × 6s (or larger), which will spread the weight over a large area and keep the platform stable. If you attach a swing or cantilevered beam to the platform, use one of these methods to hold the structure in place: fasten long screw anchors at the corners; attach structure to concrete footings; or weigh structure down with an attached sandbox.

Hardware and equipment specially designed for playgrounds can be purchased in kits or as needed. In addition to saving time, using engineered hardware is a safe method for designing critical joinery. For example, if you are wondering how many lag bolts you need to make a post/beam connection on a swingset, you'll find the easiest answer is zero if you purchase an engineered A-frame bracket instead. A-frame bracket (A), screw-in anchors (B), swing hardware (C), swing chain and seat (D), galvanized joist hangers and brackets (E), hot-dipped galvanized fasteners (F), hot-dipped glavanized eye bolt (G).

Save money by designing and building your own play structure using standard building materials and your own ingenuity.

Playset

Materials

(4) 4 × 4" post bases
(4) 8"-dia. × 2-ft. tube forms
Concrete
Landscape fabric
(1) 1 × 3" × 8 ft.
(1 lb.) 2" deck screws
(2 lb.) 2½" deck screws
(44) ⅜ × 5" carriage bolts, washers, nuts
Joist hanger brackets and nails
(8) 2¾" metal corners
(2) 1¼ × 8⅝ × 3⁹⁄₁₆" u-shaped metal straps
(6) ⅜ × 6" carriage bolts, washers, nuts
(1) ⅜ × 5" eyebolt with washer, lock washer, nut
18 ft. ¾" thick rope
Metal thimble for rope

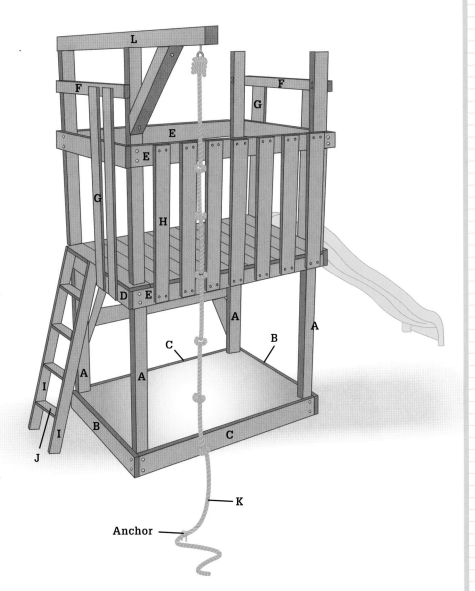

Anchor

Cutting List

Key	No.	Dimension	Material
Base & Platform			
A	4	3½ × 3½ × 10'	Pine (PT)
B	2	1½ × 7¼ × 51"	"
C	2	1½ × 7¼ × 69"	"
D	2	1½ × 5½ × 51"	"
E	4	1½ × 5½ × 58"	"
F	2	1½ × 3½ × 48"	"
G	4	5/4 × 5½ × 58"	Decking (PT)

Key	No.	Dimension	Material
H	14	5/4 × 5½ × 42"	Decking (PT)
Ladder			
I	2	1½ × 3½ × 61½"	Pine (PT)
J	4	1½ × 3½ × 17"	"
Climbing Rope			
K	1	3½ × 3½ × 7'	Pine (PT)
L	1	3½ × 3½ × 30"	"

How to Build a DIY Playset

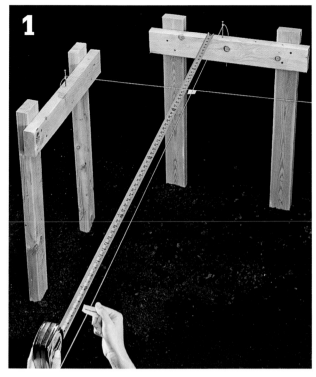

1

Lay out the project area, including the required excavation of surface materials for the buffer zone around the playset. Use batterboards and mason's string to outline the area, making sure the corners are square. Tie a second set of strings to the squared layout strings so they intersect directly over the centers of the post locations.

2

Mark digging points on the ground directly below post locations. Untie the mason's strings. *Note: Contact your local utilities company to have them mark buried gas, plumbing, or electrical lines before you start digging.*

3

Dig holes for concrete footings using a posthole digger or a power auger. Where feasible, dig at least a few inches past the frostline for your area.

4

Fill the forms with concrete, tie the mason's string back onto the batterboards and level them, and then set J-bolts into the concrete directly beneath the centers of the planned post locations.

(continued)

Set the metal post bases and washers over the bolts and hand-tighten the nuts (a standoff base is designed to elevate the post bottom to eliminate ground contact while still holding the post securely). Leave one side of the post base open so you have access with an open-end wrench to tighten each nut after trimming and aligning the post tops.

Fasten the bottoms of the posts to the standoff hardware with 10d galvanized nails, joist hanger nails or other fasteners as specified by the post base manufacturer. All predrilled guide holes in the hardware should be filled with a fastener. Plumb and brace the posts. *Note: The tops of the 4 × 4 posts should be high enough that they can all be trimmed back to final height later.*

Temporary brace

Attach 2 × 6 pressure-treated frame boards to the posts so the bottoms are level with one another and slightly above grade. Cut the 2 × 6s so they form a complete frame around the posts once installed. Use clamps and deck screws to tack the members in place until they are leveled and located exactly where you want them. After drilling the bolt guide holes, use a 1¼" spade bit to counterbore ½"-deep holes. Wrap masking tape around the spade bit to mark the ½" depth.

Install landscape fabric. To prevent weeds and grass from growing through the sand, spread landscape fabric over the ground inside the structure area and staple it to the inside surfaces of the 2 × 6 frame. Hold the top of the fabric back about 3" from the tops of the frame boards. For extra holding power, use thin wood strips as retainers for stapling or nailing the fabric.

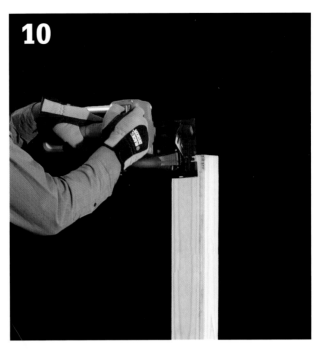

Attach the platform side boards so the tops are approximately 59" above grade. First, tack the side boards to the 4 × 4 posts with a 2½" deck screw at each end. Make sure the sides and all other members are level and plumb and then drill two bolt holes at each end for ⅜ × 5" carriage bolts. The end of each hole that will receive the nut and washer should have a 1¼"-dia. × ½" deep counterbore. Do not counterbore for carriage bolt heads. Tighten nuts onto the carriage bolts with a socket wrench or impact driver.

Trim post tops. Identify the post with the lowest post base and measure up on that post to the finished post height for the project. Mark the height and then use a laser level (or a straight board with a carpenter's level attached to it) to transfer the post top height to the other posts. After the frame and platform are installed, trim the posts along the lines. A cordless circular saw is a good tool for trimming post tops.

Add the platform support joists, using joist hanger hardware to support the 2 × 6 joist material between the side boards. Space the joists equally. The tops of the joists should be flush with the tops of the side boards.

(continued)

Cut pieces of 5/4 decking (actual thickness is 1") for the platform and install them with deck screws driven into the support joists. Arrange the boards on the joist supports first and adjust them so the gaps between boards are equal, consistent, and do not exceed ¼". Drive screws in a regular pattern, as the screwheads will be visible.

Fasten 2 × 6 railings to the posts on the sides of the structure, using ⅜ × 5" carriage bolts. The tops of the railings should be 8 ft. above ground. Counterbore the posts so the nuts and washers are recessed. Also install 2 × 4 railings on the other two sides (narrow sides) at 111" high. Paint or stain the playset with exterior-grade paint if desired.

Safety Tip ▶

For safety, add wide balusters made from deck boards to the sides. The gaps between boards should not exceed 3". Leave openings for ladders, slides, and any other accessories you wish to attach.

Fill the framed base enclosure with sand to create a sandbox (or use mulch or pea gravel, if you prefer).

How to Build a Ladder

A wooden ladder provides easy, safe access up into the fort portion of your project. This ladder is sturdy and simple to build. You'll need: (2) 2 × 4 × 61½", (4) 2 × 4 × 17", (1) 2 × 4 × 24", and (8) 2¾" metal corners.

Measure and cut the ladder standards from a pressure-treated 2 × 4. Look for tight-grained lumber with no visible defects. The steps are set at a 15° angle so they'll be level when the angled standards are set on flat ground. The back edges of the standards at the top are cut at a 75° angle.

Attach the steps. Nail one plate of each metal corner brace to the ladder sides at the correct spacing (the steps generally are 12" apart on-center) and then nail the bracket to the underside of the step using joist hanger nails.

Attach a ladder base to the bottom of the ladder to function as a spreader. Screw the 24"-long base to the bottoms of the ladder sides with deck screws, then set the ladder in place on a bed of gravel. Secure the ladder to the playset deck through the back with two deck screws per side driven into the frame.

How to Attach a Slide

A slide is perhaps the most necessary accessory for any playset. Although it is possible to build your own from scratch, the likelihood of obtaining satisfactory results is low. Any building center that carries playset parts will also sell plastic slides in many styles, colors, and sizes. You'll need a slide, three #14 × 1¼" panhead screws, a screw-in ground anchor, and a ⅜ × 1" hex bolt with washers and nuts.

Mark the slide anchor location onto the ground using a cap nail. When using a thick bed of playground mulch, raise the bottom of the slide by attaching it to a 4 × 4. This 60" slide is secured to the playset tower so the top edge is 60" above ground. To attach the slide temporarily, drive #14 × 1¼" panhead screws through the screw holes in the slide lip.

Drive an anchor for the slide base into the ground, after removing the slide, at the post marked in Step 1. The eye hook at the top should be aligned with the bolt hole in the slide.

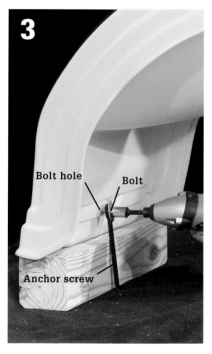

Bolt hole

Bolt

Anchor screw

Reinstall the slide, driving the fasteners through the top lip and into the playset structure. Use an exterior bolt (⅜ × 1" is used here) to attach the base of the slide to the anchor you've driven for it. The base should be resting on solid ground (not on mulch or other loose materials) or a spacer, as shown.

How to Add a Climbing Rope

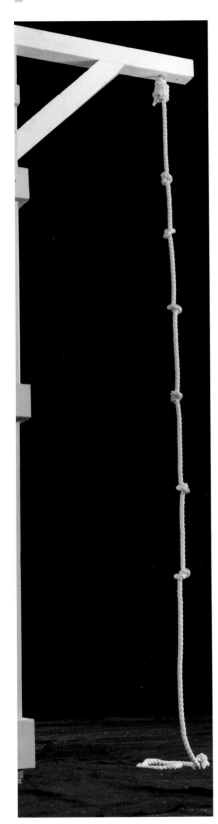

A climbing rope can be attached to a cantilevered support beam that is securely affixed to the top of your play structure.

Attach a 7-ft.-long 4 × 4 to the top of the playset structure to support a climbing rope. Use joist hanger nails and U-shaped metal straps or long metal straps to fasten the cantilevered 4 × 4 to the post tops.

Add a 4 × 4 brace with a 45° angle cut at each end. The brace is attached with a ⅜ × 6" bolt at each end and reinforced with the same U-shaped strap hardware used to attach the beam.

Hang the climbing rope. A ⅜ × 5" eyebolt can be attached to the cantilevered end of the beam, about 6" in, for an easy tie-off point. You can purchase fancier hardware, such as a swivel hook. Tie knots every foot or so in the rope for better gripping while climbing.

Anchor the bottom of the rope to a screw-in anchor or a board that's bolted to the base of the fort. The rope should not hang loose for safety reasons. If you are tying the rope to a screw-in anchor, use a large enough knot to cover the top of the anchor screw eye.

DIY Swingset

Swingsets are fairly simple projects to build, and can be anchored to a larger playset for more stability, as is the case with the model seen here. If your swingset will be freestanding, anchor all four legs with screw-in anchors. Swings can be higher or longer, as long as the A-frame supports are widely spaced and securely bolted together.

Swing seats, chains, and hardware usually come as a package. Generally, the plastic-encased chain is easier to work with and has a greater chance of success than rope, which is difficult to adjust and may stretch or loosen over time.

Swings are virtually a requirement in any playset. This swingset is bolted to a DIY playset, but it can easily be modified into a freestanding swinging structure.

Swingset

Tools & Materials

Pencil
Circular saw
Protractor
Power miter saw
Drill/driver
Sawhorses
Clamps
Stepladder
Eye and ear protection
Work gloves
(8) ⅜ × 5" carriage bolts, nuts, washers
(2) ⅜ × 6" carriage bolts, nuts, washers
(2) Swingworks A-frame brackets
   (see Resources, P. 236)
Swing seats, chains, and hardware

Cutting List

Key	No.	Dimension	Material
A	4	3½ × 3½ × 104"	Pine (PT)
B	1	3½ × 5½ × 8'	"
C	2	1½ × 5½ × 6'	"

How to Build a Swingset

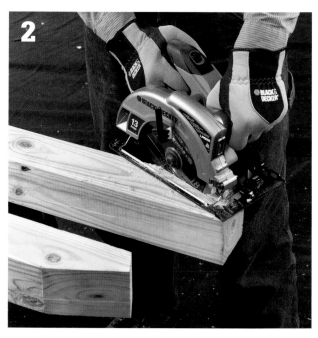

Mark the posts for cutting. If you are using A-frame brackets (strongly recommended), purchase the hardware beforehand and mark the posts using the A-frame bracket as a guide. If you are not using brackets, use a protractor or a speed square as a gauge to mark the tops of the posts at around 65° so they will meet to form a stable A-shaped structure with sufficient leg spread.

Cut the long angles on each post with a circular saw, then square off the top edge with a power miter saw or circular saw.

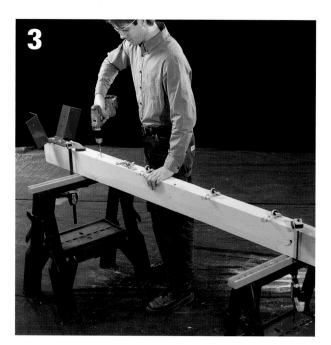

Bolt the A-frame brackets onto the 4 × 6, and then predrill the holes for the eye bolts that hold the swing. Use a long spade bit for the holes.

Assemble the legs. Lay the 4 × 4 legs for one side on a flat area, set the 4 × 6 on top of them, and then bolt the legs to the brackets. Use the fasteners recommended by the hardware manufacturer. You'll need a helper to hold the 4 × 6 steady.

5

Attach the second leg. Use a step ladder or helpers to hold the 4 × 4s steady and in place as you finish bolting into the brackets.

6

Clamp the 2 × 6 ties in position. Drill the bolt holes, and then counterbore the holes on the inside. Bolt the 2 × 6 on with 5" carriage bolts.

7

Anchor the swingset. Tack the swingset structure in place against the platform of the adjoining playset. Using a long drill bit, drill through each 4 × 4 leg and bolt the swing to the platform.

8

Hang the swings using the mounting hardware and chains or rope supplied with or recommended by the manufacturer. Test to make sure the ground clearance is adequate and adjust as necessary.

Backyard
Play Projects

Even small backyards have room for a wide variety of play structures and projects, from elaborate playhouses to simple water slides. Most of the projects in this chapter are based on traditional play—modern variations of what kids (and even grownups) have been doing for fun out in the backyard for centuries. Most of them don't have to cost a lot of money either—even the more elaborate projects can be downsized or simplified.

Some of the projects in this chapter are for small children, some are primarily for older children and some can be enjoyed by all ages. As with any project, keep safety in mind. Counterbore or bury all protruding bolts and screws, round over sharp edges, and inspect your work for places where clothes or body parts can get trapped or snagged. Apply mulch or another shock-absorbent material anywhere there's a chance of falling, because sooner or later someone will. And remember to inspect the project occasionally after it's up and in use. Bolts can loosen over time as the wood dries out and may need retightening; wood can crack and warp as it ages, creating sharp splinters; and pieces may break or come loose due to hard use.

In this chapter:

- Timberframe Sandbox
- Covered Sandbox
- Seesaw
- Zip Line
- Classic Tree Swing
- Ice Rink
- Jungle Gym
- Obstacle Course
- Swinging Rope Challenge

Timberframe Sandbox

Building this sandbox requires a good deal more effort than if you simply nailed four boards together and dumped a pile of sand in the middle. The timber construction is both charming and solid. A storage box at one end gives kids a convenient place to keep their toys. The opposite end has built-in seats, allowing children to sit above the sand as they play.

The gravel bed and landscape fabric provide a nice base for the sandbox, allowing water to drain while keeping weeds from sprouting in the sand. The gravel and liner also keep sand from migrating out of the box. The structure is set into the ground for stability and to keep the top of the pavers at ground level so you can easily mow around them. When your children outgrow the sandbox, you can turn it into a raised garden bed.

Materials ▸

(14) 4 × 4" × 8' cedar
(1) 1 × 8" × 12' cedar
(2) 1 × 6" × 8' cedar
(2) 2 × 2" × 6' cedar
Coarse gravel
Sand
Wood sealer/protectant
Heavy-duty plastic sheeting or landscape fabric
2" galvanized screws
6" galvanized barn nails or landscape spikes
Pavers (optional)
Child-safe friction hinges

If you have small children, a backyard just isn't complete without a sandbox. This version is nicely sized, sturdy, and designed for ease of cleaning.

Timberframe Sandbox

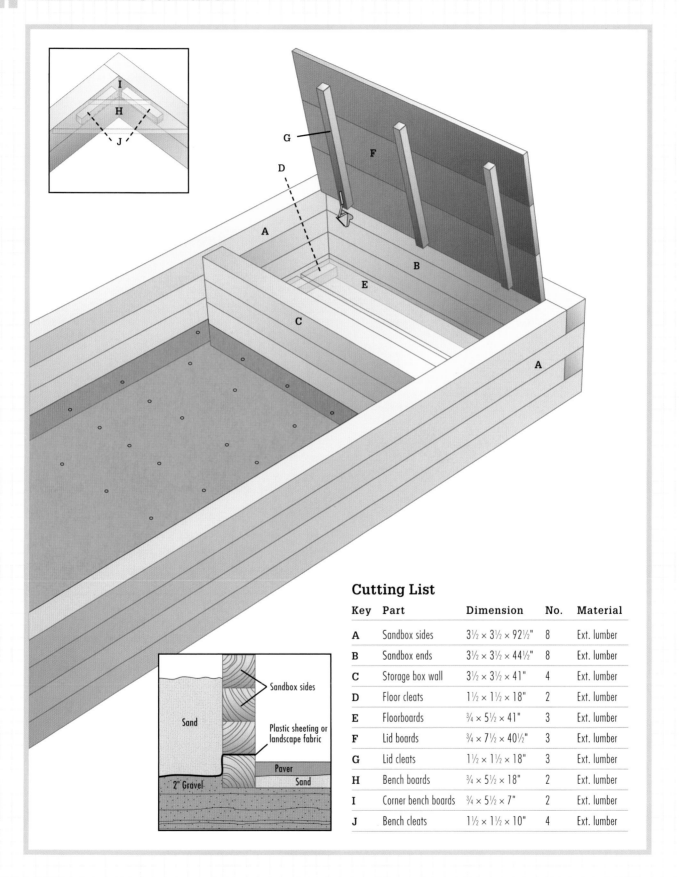

Sandbox sides

Sand

Plastic sheeting or
landscape fabric

Paver

2" Gravel

Sand

Cutting List

Key	Part	Dimension	No.	Material
A	Sandbox sides	$3\frac{1}{2} \times 3\frac{1}{2} \times 92\frac{1}{2}$"	8	Ext. lumber
B	Sandbox ends	$3\frac{1}{2} \times 3\frac{1}{2} \times 44\frac{1}{2}$"	8	Ext. lumber
C	Storage box wall	$3\frac{1}{2} \times 3\frac{1}{2} \times 41$"	4	Ext. lumber
D	Floor cleats	$1\frac{1}{2} \times 1\frac{1}{2} \times 18$"	2	Ext. lumber
E	Floorboards	$\frac{3}{4} \times 5\frac{1}{2} \times 41$"	3	Ext. lumber
F	Lid boards	$\frac{3}{4} \times 7\frac{1}{2} \times 40\frac{1}{2}$"	3	Ext. lumber
G	Lid cleats	$1\frac{1}{2} \times 1\frac{1}{2} \times 18$"	3	Ext. lumber
H	Bench boards	$\frac{3}{4} \times 5\frac{1}{2} \times 18$"	2	Ext. lumber
I	Corner bench boards	$\frac{3}{4} \times 5\frac{1}{2} \times 7$"	2	Ext. lumber
J	Bench cleats	$1\frac{1}{2} \times 1\frac{1}{2} \times 10$"	4	Ext. lumber

Timberframe Sandbox

PREPARE THE SITE

Outline a 48 × 96" area using stakes and strings. Use a shovel to remove all of the grass inside the area. Dig a flat trench that's 2" deep × 4" wide around the perimeter of the area, just inside the stakes and string (**photo 1**).

LAY THE FIRST ROW OF TIMBERS

Cut the side, end, and storage box wall timbers using a circular saw or miter saw. Coat the timbers with a wood sealer and let them dry completely. Place the first tier of sides and ends in the trench so the corners on successive rows will lap over one another. Place a level across a corner, then add or remove soil to level it. Level the other three corners the same way. Drill two ³⁄₁₆" pilot holes through the timber sides, then drive 6" barn nails through the pilot holes.

Measuring from the inside of one end, mark for the inside edge of the storage box at 18" on both sides. Align the storage box wall with the marks, making sure the corners are square, and then score the soil on either side of it. Remove the timber and dig a 3" deep trench at the score marks.

Replace the storage box timber in the trench. Its top edge must be ¾" lower than the top edge of the first tier of the sandbox wall. Add or remove dirt until the storage box timber is at the proper height. Drill ³⁄₁₆"-dia. pilot holes through the sandbox sides into the ends of the storage box timber, then drive 6" barn nails through the pilot holes.

Pour 2" of coarse gravel into the sandbox section. Compact the gravel with a hand tamper or simply by stomping on it for a while. Cover the gravel bed section with heavy-duty landscape fabric or plastic sheeting (**photo 2**). Pierce the plastic with an awl or screwdriver at 12" intervals for drainage.

BUILD THE SANDBOX FRAME

Set the second tier of timbers in place over the first tier and over the plastic sheeting, staggering the joints with the joint pattern in the first tier. Starting at the ends of the timbers, drill ³⁄₁₆"-dia. pilot holes every 24", then drive 6" galvanized barn nails through the pilot holes. Repeat for the remaining tiers of timbers, staggering the joints.

Remove the grass in the sandbox location with a flat-end spade, and then dig a trench for the first row of timbers.

Prepare the base. Lay the first row of timbers, including the wall for the storage box. Fill the sandbox area with a 2" layer of gravel, and cover with plastic sheeting.

Build the rest of the sandbox frame, staggering the corner joints. Drill holes and drive barn nails through the holes.

Attach the bench lid using heavy-duty hinges. Install a child-safe lid support to prevent the lid from falling shut.

Install 2 × 2 cleats ¾" from the top of the sandbox to support the seats in the corners. Attach the corner bench boards using galvanized screws.

Place the pavers into the sand base. Use a rubber mallet to set them in place.

Stack the remaining storage box wall timbers over the first one. Drill ³⁄₁₆"-dia. pilot holes through the sandbox sides into the ends of the storage box timbers, and then drive 6" barn nails into the pilot holes (**photo 3**). Cut the excess fabric from around the outside of the sandbox timbers using a utility knife.

BUILD THE STORAGE BOX FLOOR & LID

Cut the floor cleats and position one against each side wall along the bottom of the storage box. Attach them using 2" galvanized screws. Cut the floorboards and place them over the cleats with ½" gaps between boards to allow for drainage. Fasten the floorboards to the cleats using 2" screws.

Cut the lid boards and lay them out side-by-side, with the ends flush. Cut the lid cleats and place across the lid, one at each end and one in the middle, making sure the end of each cleat is flush with the back edge of the lid. Drill pilot holes and attach the cleats using 2" galvanized screws. Attach the lid to the sandbox frame using heavy-duty child-safe friction hinges (**photo 4**).

BUILD CORNER BENCHES

Cut the bench cleats. Mark ¾" down from the top edge of the sandbox at two corners. Align the top

edges of the bench cleats with the marks and fasten them using 2" deck screws.

Cut the corner bench boards to length with a 45° angle at each end. Place it in the corner and attach it to the cleats using 2" screws (**photo 5**). Cut the bench boards to length with a 45° angle at each end. Butt it against the corner bench board, and then attach it to the cleats. Repeat this step to install the second corner bench.

FILL SANDBOX & INSTALL BORDER

Fill the sandbox with play sand to within 4 to 6" of the top. Mark an area the width of your pavers around the perimeter of the sandbox. Remove the grass and soil in the paver area to the depth of your pavers, plus another 2", using a spade. Spread a 2" layer of sand into the paver trench. Smooth the sand level using a flat board. Tamp down. Place the pavers on top of the sand base, beginning at a corner of the sandbox (**photo 6**). Use a level or a straightedge to make sure the pavers are even and flush with the surrounding soil. If necessary, add or remove sand to level the pavers. Set the pavers in the sand by tapping them with a rubber mallet. Fill the gaps between the pavers with sand. Wet the sand lightly to help it settle. Add new sand as necessary until the gaps are filled.

Covered Sandbox

If you're looking for a fast-and-easy, down-and-dirty backyard project for kids, this sandbox is for you. At four-foot square, it is also very inexpensive to make. Simply cut the 2 × 10s to length and then attach metal corner hardware one-and-a-half inches from the ends of the 48-inch boards. Screw the 45-inch sides to the metal corners. Cut the corner seats, and then nail them to the top of each corner with casing nails. Predrill the seats before nailing to avoid splitting the wood. Finally, line the bottom with landscape fabric and fill with play sand.

A half-sheet of plywood makes a functional, if not especially attractive, sandbox cover. You can add a 1 × 2 frame and a handle in the middle to dress up the top a bit if you choose. Or, you can build a protective rollout screen that functions much like a swimming pool cover to keep debris (and neighborhood cats) out of the sandbox when it is not being used, as seen here.

This versatile sandbox couldn't be easier to build, yet it will delight kids of all ages.

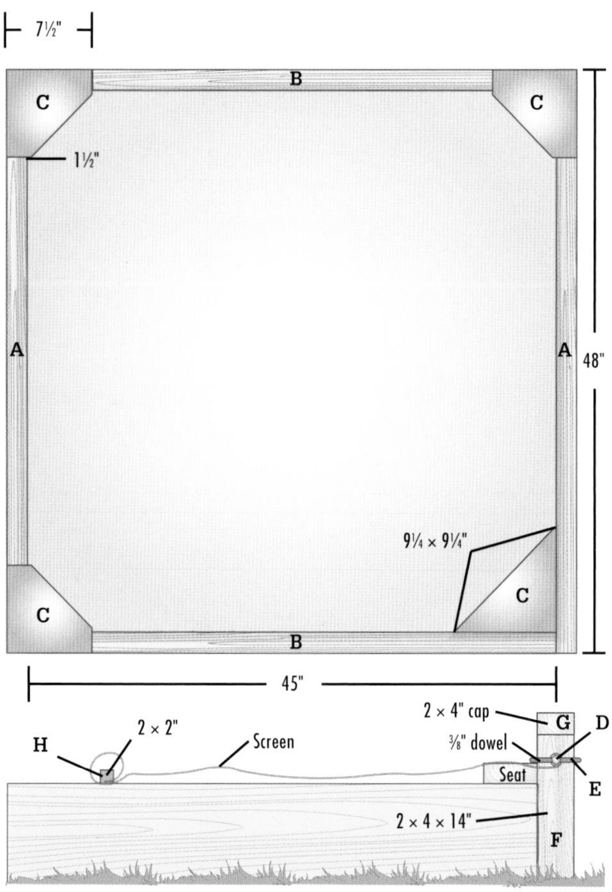

Materials & Cutting List ▸

(2) 2 × 10" × 10-ft. pressure-treated boards	Pencil
(4) 4⅞" inside metal corners (USP AC5)	**Cover:**
Deck screws (1¼, 1¾")	48 × 72" fiberglass insect mesh
16d galv. casing nails	(1) 2 × 4" × 8-ft.
Landscape fabric	(1) 1"-dia. × 54" wood dowel
Play sand	(2) ⅜"-dia. × 5" wood dowels
Circular saw	
Drill/driver	(1) 2 × 2" × 6-ft.
Framing square	

Key	Part	Dimension	No.	Material
A	Front/back	1½ × 9¼ × 48"	2	PT Pine
B	Side	1½ × 9¼ × 45"	2	PT Pine
C	Seat	1½ × 9¼ × 9¼"	4	PT Pine
D	Cover roller	1 × 54"	1	Wood dowel
E	Roller pins	⅜ × 5"	2	Wood dowel
F	Roller supports	1½ × 3½ × 14"	2	2 × 4
G	Roller cap	1½ × 3½ × 51"	1	2 × 4
H	Tack strip	1½ × 1½ × 48"	1	2 × 2

Diagram labels: 7½", C, B, C, 1½", A, A, 48", 9¼ × 9¼", C, C, B, 45", 2 × 2", H, Screen, 2 × 4" cap, G, D, ⅜" dowel, Seat, E, 2 × 4 × 14", F

How to Build a Covered Sandbox

Cut the front, back, and sides to length from 2 × 10 pressure-treated stock and then join the corners with metal connectors and 1¼" screws. Use a framing square to make sure the corners are square.

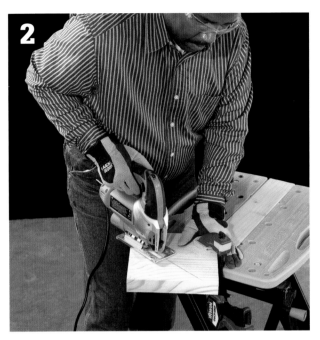

Cut four 9¼"-long pieces of 2 × 10 to make the sandbox seatboards. Mark a cutting line 1½" from the corner on two adjoining sides, and then connect the ends of the cutting lines with a straightedge to make the angled cutting line. Make the angled cut with a jigsaw or handsaw if your power miter saw doesn't have enough cutting capacity.

Make the cover. Cut a piece of insect mesh (or very light-gauge hardware cloth) to 47 × 60". Look for the type that says "Animal Resistant." Fold a hem into one edge on the 47" side and staple it to the 1"-dia. × 54" wood dowel, centered end-to-end. Fold a hem along the opposite edge and staple it to a 48"-long 2 × 2 tack strip. Install seats.

Tack strip

Cover roller

Install the cover. Attach the 2 × 4 sides and cap at one end of the sandbox. The roller should be fitted into the 1⅛" guide holes in the side supports during assembly. Drill ⅜" holes ½" from the ends of the roller dowel and glue 5"-long pieces of ⅜"-dia. doweling into the holes for roller handles. Paint all wood parts or coat with a protective, UV-resistant stain.

Seesaw

For kids, the seesaw (also called a teeter-totter) is both enjoyable recreation and a good introduction to simple machines and basic physics. It's a revelation for a child to be able to lift a huge grownup off the ground just by having them sit closer to the pivot point.

A seesaw can be as basic as a board laid across a log, or it may be an elaborate wooden construction perfectly balanced on a pivot point that rotates in any direction while going up and down. If you design your own seesaw, experiment with it on graph paper before building it. Draw different combinations of pivot point heights and board lengths; then see what happens when the board goes down. Small changes in height and length can mean the difference between a three-foot drop and a six-foot drop, changing a gentle kid-friendly seesaw into a seesaw that terrifies (or thrills) adults.

Make sure the pivot point is solid, either by building a wide, stable base or by embedding the supporting posts in at least two feet of concrete. Lock the seesaw board onto the pipe or dowel that it pivots on (for example, with pipe strap)—otherwise it can bounce off the pipe.

Materials ▶

Premixed concrete	Pipe joint compound
Gravel	Handles (conduit fittings)
Lumber	⅜ × 8" galvanized
Mulch	carriage bolts with
Exterior wood glue	nuts and washers
Circular Saw	Galvanized pipe
2½" deck screws	& fittings

Whether you call it a seesaw or a teeter-totter, this venerable plaything has been a fixture for thousands of years, and almost every culture has developed a version of it. All you need to make one is a long board and a center pivot.

Seesaw

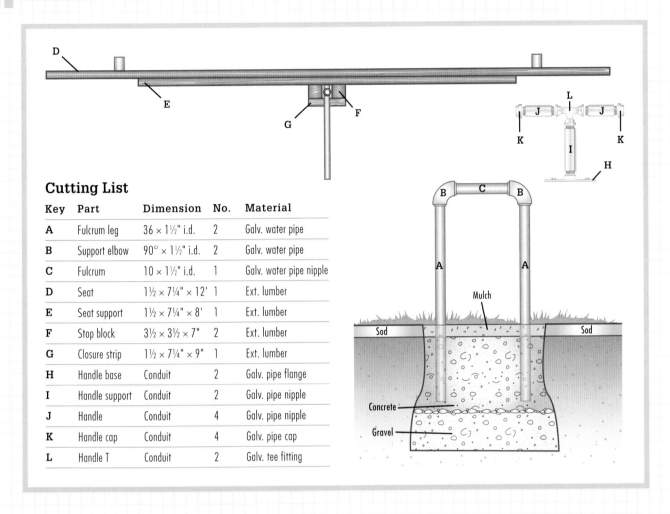

Cutting List

Key	Part	Dimension	No.	Material
A	Fulcrum leg	36 × 1½" i.d.	2	Galv. water pipe
B	Support elbow	90° × 1½" i.d.	2	Galv. water pipe
C	Fulcrum	10 × 1½" i.d.	1	Galv. water pipe nipple
D	Seat	1½ × 7¼" × 12'	1	Ext. lumber
E	Seat support	1½ × 7¼" × 8'	1	Ext. lumber
F	Stop block	3½ × 3½ × 7"	2	Ext. lumber
G	Closure strip	1½ × 7¼" × 9"	1	Ext. lumber
H	Handle base	Conduit	2	Galv. pipe flange
I	Handle support	Conduit	2	Galv. pipe nipple
J	Handle	Conduit	4	Galv. pipe nipple
K	Handle cap	Conduit	4	Galv. pipe cap
L	Handle T	Conduit	2	Galv. tee fitting

A wide, stable base allows you to set up this seesaw on any level area. Seesaws large enough to be used by several children at a time are available from online suppliers, and can be assembled with standard hand tools.

Order a Seesaw Online ▸

If you're not sure you want to build your own seesaw, or if you want a seesaw that's not fixed in place, many other models are available from retailers and online suppliers. (See Resources on page 236, or just search for Seesaws.) You can also order plans, then use your own wood.

How to Build a Seesaw

Build the fulcrum assembly from 1½" (inside diameter) galvanized steel water pipe. Tighten a pair of 90° elbows to the threaded ends of a 10" nipple. Use a pipe wrench to crank them at least a full turn past hand-tight. Use pipe joint compound or Teflon tape to lubricate the threads so you can tighten the fitting more easily. Add a 36" section of water pipe to the open end of each elbow.

Set the fulcrum assembly into concrete. Build a 2 × 4 brace to support the assembly while the concrete hardens. The ends of the fulcrum legs should extend 14" into the concrete, making the top of the assembly approximately 24" above grade. After digging the hole for the fulcrum, widen the base on all sides to create a bell shape for extra stability.

Pour concrete into the hole. Add 2 to 4" of drainage gravel (such as 1-2" river rock) to the bottom of the hole before pouring the concrete. Smooth the concrete surface with a trowel, forming a crown so water doesn't collect.

Make the seesaw board. The seesaw board is created from a pair of 2 × 8s that are fastened together face-to face with construction adhesive and screws. Glue and screw the 2 × 8s together, then mark the center and outside diameter of the pipe on the bottom board.

Glue and bolt 4 × 4 stop blocks to the seesaw board so they fit around both sides of the pipe, which should fit snugly between the blocks. Use two ⅜" × 8" carriage bolts for each side, making sure the bolt head is on the top (longer) 2 × 8 and the bolt is fastened on the bottom side (shorter).

Place the seesaw board onto the pipe at the top of the fulcrum assembly. Then attach a wood closure strip beneath the fulcrum bar to lock the seatboard in position.

Apply the finishing touches. Sand the boards using up to 150-grit sandpaper for a smooth finish that will resist splintering. You may make small arched cutouts on both edges near the seatboard ends if you wish to create a classic seesaw detail. Attach a sturdy handle 18 to 24" from each end. Use very large door pulls or custom-make the handles—the ones seen here are made by fabricating rigid conduit and fittings into a T-shape (see page 71). Apply a protective finish (clear sealer or paint) to all wood surfaces. Occasionally lubricate the top bar in the fulcrum with graphite spray to improve performance and decrease noise.

Zip Line

A zip line is a simple contraption consisting of a seat or handle hanging from a heavy-duty pulley that is suspended from a steel cable. The cable is tied between a pair of trees, posts, or other sturdy structures you can find or build—as long as one is higher than the other. If you're starting the cable from a treehouse or platform, make sure any framing that the eyebolt attaches to is rock-solid.

A zip line can be slow, gentle, and close enough to the ground to push off and stop yourself with your feet. Or, it can be very high and very fast, carrying you down mountainsides or across lakes, rivers, and canyons. The longest known zip line is 1.2 miles, drops almost 1,000 feet, and reaches speeds of up to 100 miles per hour. These "extreme" zip lines should be created by professionals only and used under the supervision of a qualified professional.

You can create a smaller, safer version of that mind-bending ride in your own backyard with a length of steel cable, some long eyebolts, and a zip line kit with a heavy-duty tandem pulley. Do not use the standard pulleys sold at hardware stores for zip lines—they're not meant for this application. Similarly, use only braided cable (usually stainless steel) that has been specifically selected and packaged for a zip line. You'll find a number of purveyors of zip line products on the Internet (see Resources, page 236).

Materials ▸

Heavy-duty, exterior-rated eyebolts, washers and nuts	Discarded tire
	¾" turnbuckle
	Mulch
(2) Metal thimbles for cable	Rubber mallet
	Drill with spade bits and bit extender
(6) Stainless steel cable clamps	Zip line kit

A zip line is a braided metal cable stretched from a point of access to a point of lower elevation. Add a pulley and a tow bar or handlebars and let the joy rides start.

Safety Tip ▸

Minimum safety equipment when using a zip line in a dangerous area includes: Harness, helmets, shoulder- and knee-pads, and other safety equipment, as required.

A kit and a few basic tools are all you need to install a zip line. Be sure to buy heavy-duty stainless steel or galvanized fittings (kits are available from online suppliers).

Zip Line Requirements ▸

For a good ride, make the zip line at least 75 feet long, with a minimum slope of five feet. Trees must be heathy and at least 10 inches in diameter. If you're starting at a treehouse or platform, reinforce the framing with additional fasteners or metal brackets.

Test the run before drilling the holes. Wrap the cable around the trees, secure it with cable clamps and hold it in position at the level where the eyebolt will be attached with wood clamps or large nails. Then tie a heavy sandbag to the handle so it's hanging where a person would be and send it down the cable. If it seems too slow or fast, move one end of the cable to compensate. Watch for obstacles in the path of the cable, and cut branches back four feet on all sides.

Zip Lines in Motion

Lighter-duty zipline kits made for use by children are sold in relatively inexpensive kits. Their maximum distances traveled range from 30 to 90 ft.

A high-adventure zip line requires a very unusual backyard with tall trees and ample space, as shown here. But setting up a slightly tamer run from your deck to the old maple tree is a great way for active people of all ages to learn and develop skills.

How to Install a Zip Line

Drill a hole through the center of each tree (high end and low end) for an eyebolt. The holes should be the same diameter as the eyebolt shaft. You'll need to use an extra-long spade bit or a bit extender to clear a tree trunk, which should be at least 10" in diameter.

Insert an eyebolt (stainless steel or triple-dipped galvanized) through the guide hole and then secure it to the tree with a wide washer, such as a fender washer, and a nut. The end of the bolt should protrude 1 to 2" past the tree. Inspect the nut periodically to make sure it is still tight.

Attach a turnbuckle to the eyebolt on the low end of the cable run. The turnbuckle should be sized and rated for the cable size, the total span and the maximum weight load of your zip line.

Loop the cable (use only braided, stainless steel cable rated for zip line usage) through the eyebolt on the high side, place a metal thimble at the loop, and then secure it in place with three cable clamps.

Thread the cable through an old tire that will be positioned at the end of the run (on the downhill side) to work as a brake that prevents zip line riders from crashing into the tree or structure where the cable is secured. First, drill centered guide holes for the cable in opposite sides of an old, nonsteel-belted rubber tire. Also drill several ½" holes at the bottom of the tire tread to allow for water drainage.

Secure the cable to the turnbuckle at the low end. The turnbuckle should be loosened almost all the way so you can tighten the cable. Pull the cable through the turnbuckle as tightly as you can, and then lock it in place with three cable clamps. Test the tension in the cable, and tighten the turnbuckle, as needed.

Clip the handle or trolley onto the cable according to the manufacturer's instructions and test out the zip line, taking care to follow all safety precautions.

Launching Pads ▶

If your yard doesn't have much natural slope you'll have to create the slope to make your zip line work. You can do this by attaching the high end of the line to a tree or structure with a higher access point, such as a second-level deck. Or, you can build a launching platform on the tree for the high spot. A launching pad with ladder access is a fairly easy project to build and will create a safe entry point for zipline users. See page 191 for information on treehouse-type platforms.

Classic Tree Swing

A rope hung from a large tree may be a simple swinging apparatus, but kids and even adults will find it completely irresistible. The rope may be hung with just a knot at the bottom for gripping or it may support a swing seat or an old tire.

All that is really required to build a rope swing is a healthy tree, a length of heavy rope, and the ability to tie a good knot. Use ½-inch diameter or larger rope (larger is better) made of nylon or hemp. Tie a few knots in the bottom of the rope as grips and to prevent unraveling, even if you plan to add a swing seat. Watch the rope for signs of wear, and test it often. Make sure smaller children understand how to use it safely, and that they should never make loops in it.

When siting your swing, look for a tree that has a sturdy limb at least eight inches in diameter and nearly horizontal. The limb should be at least 10 feet above ground and the swinging area should be free and clear of all obstacles, including the tree trunk, which should be at least six feet from the point where the swing is tied (further if the rope is longer than ten feet). Landing and access areas should be clear of hazards and have shock-absorbing mulch or ground cover. Do not allow small children to use the swing without adult supervision.

Tools & Materials ▸

½"-dia. rope or larger (nylon or hemp)
⅝"-dia. hot-dipped galvanized eyebolt
    with washer and nut
Metal thimble (to match rope)
Old tire (optional) or swing
Drill and spade bit for eye bolt
Stepladder
Eye and ear protection
Work gloves

A tree swing can be installed practically anywhere that you have a tree, clear swinging area, and safe spots for landing and access.

How to Hang a Tree Swing

Attach a ⅝" galvanized eyebolt through the center of a branch that's at least 8" in diameter. Insert a thimble through the eye bolt; then tie the rope onto the eyebolt, threading it through the thimble to make the top curve. This is a tree-friendly approach to hanging a swing

Option: Tie the rope to the tree. If the branch is too high to easily reach with a ladder, throw a small cord with a weight over the branch, then use it to pull the rope up. Tie a loop in the end of the rope and pull it tight. Test the knot to make sure it is secure and does not slip. *Note: wrapping a rope or chain around a tree limb is okay as a short-term swinging solution, but it can actually cause more long-term harm to the tree than an eyebolt. Prolonged friction from a tight rope can eventually start to strangle the limb by cutting through the bark.*

Rope Selection ▸

Use ½"-dia. or larger nylon or hemp rope for a rope swing. Hemp is a traditional rope for swings, but will eventually start to rot if left out year round. Nylon is almost indestructible, but will stretch slightly and is more expensive than hemp. Nylon is available in fun colors. A 12" galvanized steel eyebolt with thimble inserted into the eye offers a safe, tree-friendly hanging method.

Hang the tire or swing seat. Swings are an excellent use for an old tire, but avoid steel-belted types with exposed steel strands, and clean the tire thoroughly before using it. Drill large holes in the tread of the tire to drain water away (inset). Do not use hard objects or objects with sharp corners (such as wood planks) as tree swings—they can cause damage or injury.

Ice Rink

The hockey-playing regions of the world boast a long tradition of flooding backyards during the winter to create personal ice rinks where neighborhood kids (and adults) can practice their skating and hockey skills. Although flooding even a small rink requires a considerable amount of water, the costs are not excessive unless you happen to live in an area with water consumption restrictions. A backyard rink is always available and you control the maintenance quality when it comes to keeping it smooth and snow-free.

Although it's possible to create a rink on bare ground using snow banks to create a border, this doesn't work well in areas that experience occasional warm periods during the winter when everything melts away. To keep the water contained so it can refreeze instead of soaking into thawed ground, install wood walls all the way around the rink and line the ground with a wide sheet of six-mil poly sheeting (available at home centers) or other waterproof membrane.

To resurface the ice when it gets rough, shovel off all snow and ice chips and then use a hose to spray the entire surface with a coating of water that will melt and smooth the ice.

Perhaps the best reason for making your own ice rink in your own yard is that it makes supervising children, which should always be done, more convenient.

Materials for building a backyard skating rink include: ¾" plywood strips for the sidewalls; 2 × 6 lumber to make wall bracing; plastic sheeting for a moisture membrane; foam pipe insulation sleeve to provide padding for the sidewall top edges.

Tools & Materials ▸

Plastic sheeting	Circular saw or
2 × 6 lumber	power miter saw
¾" CDX plywood	Hose
Deck screws	Water
(1⅝, 2½")	Mending plates
Foam pipe	or gussets
insulation sleeves	Insulation tape
6" spikes	Eye and ear
Drill/driver	protection
Clamps	Work gloves

A backyard ice rink gives the whole family a good reason to get out of the house during the winter.

Making a Backyard Ice Rink

Cut plywood panels for the sidewalls from ¾" plywood—preferably exterior grade plywood such as CDX. You can make the walls anywhere from 8 to 48" high, depending on the slope of your yard, your budget, and how serious you are about playing hockey. If your rink will include a hockey goal or goals, consider installing a higher wall behind the goals to serve as a backstop.

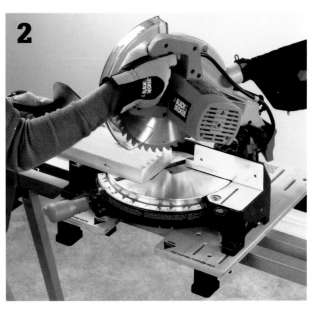

Cut sidewall braces from 2 × 6 stock—preferably pressure-treated lumber. The braces should have a 45° angle at each end. Cut enough braces so you have one for every two feet of sidewall.

Assemble the sidewall sections. Make enough 8- and 4-ft.-long sections to encircle the rink. Use 2½" deck screws to attach the braces to 2 × 6 base plates, and use 1⅝" deck screws to attach the sidewall panels to the vertical edges of the braces. Keep the braces a few inches away from the ends of each section so you can join sections with mending plates or gussets where seams occur.

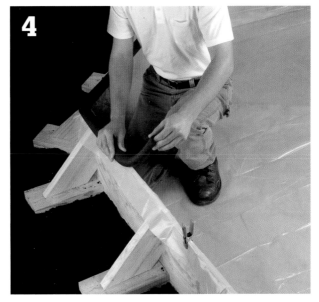

Arrange the sidewall sections around the perimeter of your skating rink area. Drive a couple of 6" spikes through each base plate to hold it in place and attach plywood gussets or mending plates over each seam between sections. Lay plastic sheeting over the area to be flooded, with the edges draped over the sidewalls. Cushion the edges by snapping foam pipe insulation sleeves over the tops. Do not use fasteners to attach the sheeting. If you need to seam the sheeting, use insulation tape. Fill the area with at least 2" of water, and then let it freeze; refresh, as necessary.

Jungle Gym

The first known jungle gym—a framework of bamboo cubes—was developed by a mathematician as a way of teaching his children about three-dimensional space. It never caught on as a teaching aid, but eventually became quite popular on playgrounds and has since become the progenitor for a wide variety of climbing structures.

Although earlier mass-marketed playground versions of jungle gyms were made from welded metal, most jungle gyms for home use today are constructed of wood or a combination of wood and metal. Because playground falls are not uncommon, it's recommended that you line the area beneath the jungle gym with a thick layer of mulch (see page 27). Sand any rough, splintery areas and round over all sharp edges before you assemble the jungle gym.

This jungle gym is made from scratch using pressure-treated lumber held together with lag bolts. Because the chemicals used to treat lumber these days are very corrosive, be sure to use triple-dipped zinc plated or stainless steel bolts, washers, and nuts.

The climbing rungs (monkey bars) on this jungle gym are made from 1" inside-diameter galvanized water pipe. If you'd rather not cut all that pipe, you can buy prefabricated monkey bars at just about any larger building center and several Internet stores. The assembly process we used is fairly straightforward: you simply create the six wood frames that make up the structure and then bolt them together, with the monkey-bar "ladder" connecting the two large side frames. Small children should use the jungle gym only under careful adult supervision.

Materials ▸

2 × 4 ext. lumber	1¼" o.d. galvanized
4 × 4	water pipe (or
2½" deck screws	monkey bar kit)
Carriage bolts with	(3) ⅜"-dia. × 33"
washers and	threaded rod with
nuts (⅜ × 2½",	nuts/washers
⅜ × 4½", ⅜ × 5")	Sandpaper

Climbing never gets old. This jungle gym is simple to build but challenging enough to keep the kids busy for hours.

Jungle Gym

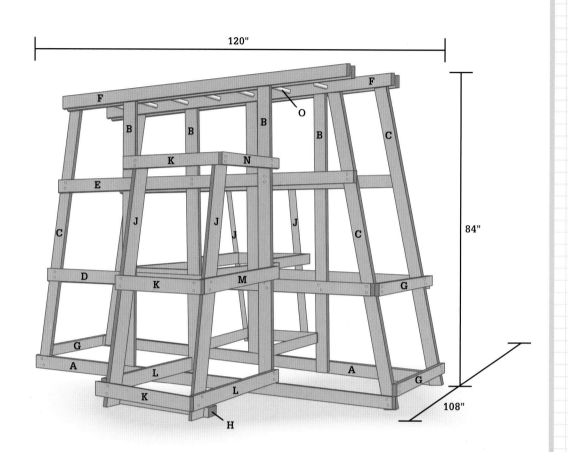

Cutting List

Key	Dimension	No.
A	3½ × 3½ × 120"	2
B	1½ × 3½ × 84"	6
C	1½ × 3½ × 86"	4
D	1½ × 3½ × 111¾"	2
E	1½ × 3½ × 100½"	2
F	1½ × 3½ × 96"	4
G	1½ × 3½ × 36"	4
H	3½ × 3½ × 33"	2

Key	Dimension	No.
J	1½ × 3½ × 61½"	4
K	1½ × 3½ × 30"	6
L	1½ × 3½ × 37½"	4
M	1½ × 3½ × 32¼"	4
N	1½ × 3½ × 26¼"	4
O	1¼ o.d. × 29" galv. water pipe	7
P	⅜ × 33" threaded rod	3

*All lumber is exterior-rated.

How to Build a Jungle Gym

Start by cutting all of the rails and uprights for the six frames to length. The ends of the outer uprights and the intermediate rails are cut at a 12° angle. After cutting and before assembly, thoroughly sand all of the parts to eliminate any slivers, rounding over any sharp edges as you sand.

Assemble the frames. The jungle gym structure is composed of six frames that are built individually and then squared and bolted together. Start with the large side frames, laying out the rails and uprights so the distances between rails are equal. Tack each joint with a single 2½" deck screw.

Lay out the carriage bolt locations once the frames are tacked together and squared. Use two bolts per joint. We used several lengths of ⅜"-dia., triple-dipped carriage bolts with the heads oriented on the outside faces of the frames. Joints where two 2 × 4s are assembled face-to-face require 2½" bolts; joints where a 2 × 4 is laid flat against the edge of another 2 × 4 require 4½" bolts. Mark the holes on the nut side of the joint.

Drill counterbores for the washers at the drilling points marked on the nut side of each joint. Mark a ½" drilling depth for each counterbore hole. Once the counterbores are all drilled, drill ⅜"-dia. guide holes through the counterbore centers using a spade bit. Drill all the way through the workpieces.

(continued)

5

Insert a carriage bolt through each guide hole, thread on a washer, and attach a nut. Attach all nuts in each frame, tightening by hand only. Once the entire structure is assembled and squared, then you should go in and tighten all nuts fully. Join the frames with carriage bolts driven through counterbored guide holes. The uprights in the large side frames are attached to 4 × 4 skids—use ⅜ × 5" triple-dipped bolts.

6

Build and attach the wing assemblies to the side frames as shown in the diagram. These assemblies are good for climbing, but they provide an even more important function in stabilizing the jungle gym structure.

7

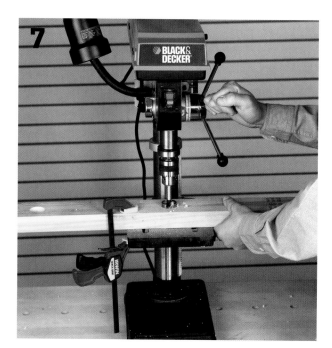

Drill set holes for the monkey bars. Mark drilling centers for the monkey bars on the inside faces of two 2 × 4 upper rails. The holes should be spaced 12" apart on-center. Mount a 1¼" Forstner bit in your drill press and set the drilling depth to 1". Drill the holes for the monkey bars. If you do not have access to a drill press, you can use a hand drill with a 1¼" spade bit.

8

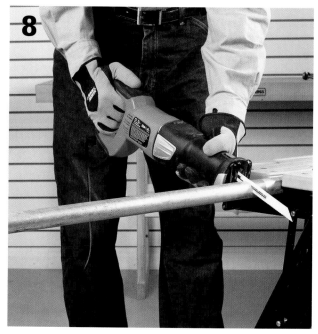

Cut the monkey bars to length from 1¼" outside diameter galvanized water pipe. The best and safest tool for this is a metal cutoff saw, but you can also use a metal-cutting bade mounted in a reciprocating saw. Be sure to secure the pipe before cutting.

9

Install the monkey bars in the upper-rail guide holes and clamp the rails together with bar or pipe clamps. Fit the assembly between the side frames and clamp the parts together. Attach the rails to the outer rails with carriage bolts installed through both rails and the uprights between the rails. Use ⅜ × 4½" carriage bolts.

10

Cut and install 2 × 4 filler strips to fit between the top ends of the uprights, sandwiched between the horizontal frame tops. The main purpose of these fillers is to eliminate pinching hazards where small hands can fit.

11

Install 33"-long pieces of threaded rod at each end and in the middle to draw the "ladder" sides together. Drill guide holes for the all-thread so they fit inside rungs and fasten with nuts and washers set into counterbores. Tighten the nuts evenly so the "ladder" doesn't rack. Do not overtighten.

12

Add the ladder steps between the side frames to create access to the monkey bars. Once all the parts are installed and the structure fits together squarely, use a cordless impact driver or a ratchet wrench to fully tighten all of the nuts onto the carriage bolts.

Obstacle Course

Children enjoy physical challenges, and a simple obstacle course full of opportunities to run, jump, balance, climb, and get very dirty can keep them busy and occupied for hours.

Very loosely inspired by Army basic training exercises (exceptas of the obstacles to make the course bigger and more complicated, or come up with your own ideas. Use playground mulch or rubber mats where kids will be landing to avoid injuries. Sand and round over any sharp edges.

An obstacle course is a fun introduction to competition for your youngsters. You only need a few items to create a course that encourages kids to become and stay active. A typical back-yard course is a blend of built, purchased, and found obstacles.

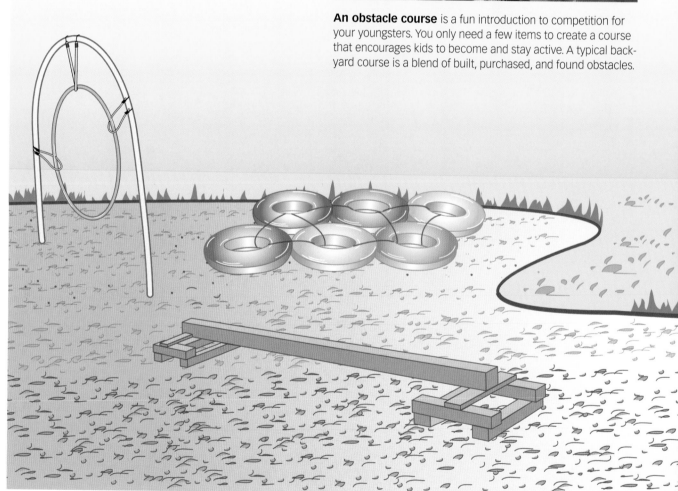

One of the best features of a good obstacle course is that you can change it around regularly to keep your kids on their toes. Add and subtract new features, rearrange the order and spacing of the obstacles, and find ways to build in new surprises that keep the course from becoming dull and predictable. It's okay to present the course as a timed race, but be sure it is done in the spirit of sportsmanship, and if conflicts or disappointment happen treat them as teaching moments. As with any play event, do not let your young children run the course unsupervised.

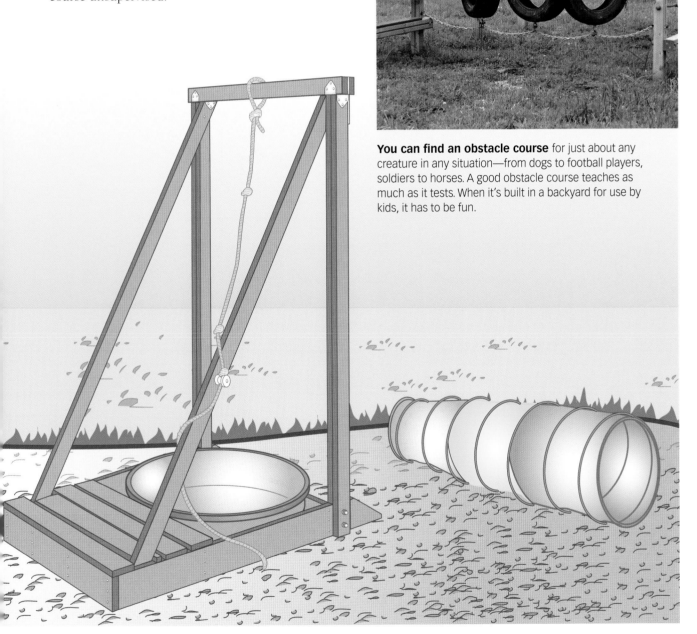

You can find an obstacle course for just about any creature in any situation—from dogs to football players, soldiers to horses. A good obstacle course teaches as much as it tests. When it's built in a backyard for use by kids, it has to be fun.

Elements of an Obstacle Course

Limbo. Run a piece of string with bells hanging from it between trees or stakes, about 1½ ft. off the ground. The goal is to crawl underneath the string as quickly as you can without ringing any bells.

Tire Run. The classic test for fancy footwork is a series of old tires rigged together in two rows of three or more. This traditional obstacle, used by football teams and the Green Berets alike, can be made by fastening old tires (avoid steel-belted radials) together with nuts and bolts. For a lighter-duty version of the Tire Run that doesn't result in a half dozen old tires living in your yard or garage year-round, substitute inflatable swimming rings (36"-dia. works well) and lash them together with bungee cords.

Play Tunnel. Although you can make DIY versions of a play tunnel using large tubular concrete forms, you're much better off purchasing an expandable play tunnel from a department store to add a fun element to your obstacle course. Costing around $30, these simple toys are suitable for indoor use as well.

Hoop Jump. Make a hula-hoop jump with a 10-ft. length of ¾"-dia. PVC tubing and two 18" pieces of ½" CPVC tubing. Drive the CPVC stakes into the ground 40" apart, with 6" sticking up above ground. Slip the open ends of the ¾" tubing over the stakes so the pipe curves into an inverted U shape. Buy a hulahoop (28"-dia. is standard) and hang it, centered, from the tubing with bungee cords. Lay a bed of rubber mulch around the hoop so you can dive and roll through.

Other Obstacles. Just in this book you'll find a number of additional fun projects that can be incorporated into an obstacle course. They include a zip line, left (page 74), a swinging rope challenge, middle (page 92), and a jungle gym, right (page 82).

Balance Beam. Make the central beam out of an 8-ft.-long 4 × 6 timber. Attach a 16"-long 2 × 4 crosspiece to each end of the beam with 16d nails or deck screws. Set the beam on top of a stack of four 16"-long 4 × 4 blocks to support the balance beam. Nail all the pieces together to keep them from shifting.

A rope swing can be hung from a tree branch or another structure in the obstacle course area (see page 78), or you can build a portable, self-contained swinging structure (page 92).

Swinging Rope Challenge

Long before Tarzan movies showed us the excitement of swinging from tree to tree, kids used rope swings as a fun way to exercise and to compete. A swinging rope that offers clearance over a dreaded hazard has been a staple of the obstacle course, whether the contestants are knights errant, soldiers, football players, or on a reality TV show. The portable rope stand seen here is designed to accommodate a 48-inch diameter kids' pool that can be filled with water, mud, or perhaps a more creative "hazard." Kids launch themselves from the small deck, swing over the pool, and then let go and land in soft sand or on a gym mat. If you don't paint the structure, build it with pressure-treated (PT) lumber.

Tools & Materials ▸

(4) 2 × 8" × 8 ft. PT
(7) 2 × 4" × 8 ft. PT
(2) 2 × 4" × 10 ft. PT
(2) 8 ft. deck boards
(8) ⅜ × 3" lag bolts
    with washers
    and nuts
Deck screws (2", 3")
(2) Post cap hardware
Joist hanger nails
Rope
Sand mats or mulch

36 to 48"-dia. play
    wading pool
Spool
Power saw
Drill/driver
Construction adhesive
Clamps
Pencil
Ruler
Hammer
Eye and ear protection
Work gloves

Grab the knotted rope and swing across the pool of water for some jungle-inspired fun.

Swinging Rope Challenge

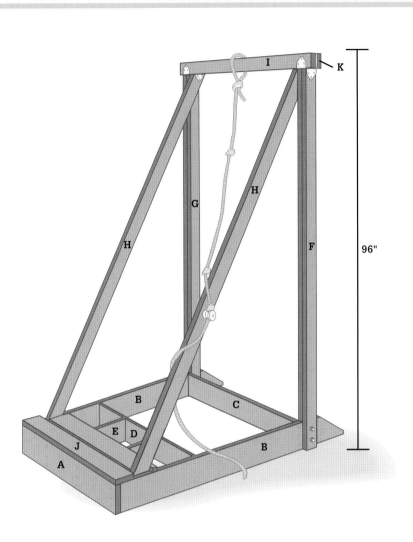

96"

Cutting List

Key	Part	Dimension	No.	Material
A	Base end	1½ × 7½ × 48"	1	2 × 8
B	Base side	1½ × 7½ × 72"	2	2 × 8
C	Spacer	1½ × 3½ × 45"	1	2 × 4
D	Deck rim	1½ × 7½ × 45"	1	2 × 8
E	Deck joist	1½ × 7½ × 21"	4	2 × 8
F	Outer upright	1½ × 3½ × 96"	2	2 × 4
G	Inner upright	1½ × 3½ × 88½"	2	2 × 4
H	Diagonal	1½ × 3½ × 113"	2	2 × 4
I	Beam	1½ × 3½ × 54"	2	2 × 4
J	Deck board	⁵⁄₄ × 5½ × 48"	4	Decking
K	Beam spacer	¾ × 3½ × 54"	1	Plywood

How to Build a Swinging Rope Challenge

Make the base. Start by cutting the base sides to length and cutting an angled profile at the front end of each part. Join the base end to the sides with 3" deck screws. Add the 2 × 4 spacer at the front, a few inches in from the profiled ends of the base. Attach the deck joists to the base end and then attach the deck rim to the ends of the joists.

Install the uprights. Cut the inner and outer upright pairs to length and attach them together with glue and 3" deck screws. Set each assembly onto the top edge of the base, 12" in from the front (profiled) end. Attach each post with a pair of counterbored ⅜ × 3" lag bolts.

Mark and cut the diagonal braces. Place a 10-ft. 2 × 4 in position so one end fits into the back inside end of the base and the other crosses the top of each upright post. Mark cutting lines on the 2 × 4s, cut to length, and angle according to your cutting lines. Fasten the braces with lag bolts.

Install the beam. Attach adjustable post caps to the tops of the inner and outer uprights and then fasten them to the uprights with joist hanger nails. Cut a beam to length from doubled 2 × 4s and set it onto the postcap saddles. Adjust the movable half of the cap and secure all parts. Insert a ½" plywood spacer between 2 × 4 beam halves and secure into a fixed post cap.

Cut deck boards to length and screw them down onto the deck joists. Make cutouts to fit around the diagonal braces if needed. There should be a gap of ¼" between deck boards.

Tie the swinging rope securely to the top beam and tie a knot or two into the rope for grabbing points. Attach an empty thread spool or another object to the outside face of a diagonal brace to make a resting point for the rope so it can be reached from the deck.

Water Slides ▸

If your kids would rather be found in the water than swinging over it, you can make your own water-park style water slide with only a roll of plastic sheeting and a hose. Buy a roll of 6-mil, 10-foot wide (or larger) polyethylene sheeting. Roll it out and unfold it, preferably on a slope if you have one. Consider weighing down the edges with pieces of wood or other heavy objects so the plastic doesn't blow away (make sure wood is sanded smooth and finished to avoid splinters). Then, turn the hose on and spray water over the length of the plastic. The water will be cold at first, but it warms up quickly on the plastic. Add baby shampoo liberally, both on the plastic and on yourself; then take a running start and dive onto the plastic. Dish soap will also work, but baby shampoo doesn't sting if you get it in your eyes.

Sports & Games

Backyard sports and games are not just for kids. Be they serious, competitive games or sloppy, disorganized fun, the point is to play; the more you play, the more exercise you'll get and the healthier you'll be. And most backyard games and courts will fit easily into small- to medium-sized yards. Some games like ladder golf, beanbag toss, bocce, horseshoes, and pickleball can even be squeezed onto a sidewalk or driveway.

Backyards offer many opportunities for fun and games and even organized contests. If you are enthusiastic about golf, softball, racquet sports, or skateboarding, you can outfit your yard as a practice facility. If you add a golf net you can practice your drive all day in a space not much larger than a large walk-in closet. Basketball and tennis skills also can be developed on small backyard courts. Many of these sports activities can also share the same space. Sports courts, which are made from thin plastic tiles laid on a concrete slab, are an outstanding example of combining uses.

All of the projects in this section can be built with standard construction tools and average skills, except for the sports court, which involves extensive concrete work.

Costs and time to build vary widely for these projects, but all of them reward the effort because all of them create compelling reasons to get outside.

In this chapter:

- Skateboard Ramp
- Basketball Hoop
- Bocce Court
- Batting Cage
- Golf Net
- Horseshoe Pit
- Multi-use Sports Court
- Tetherball
- Pickleball
- Putting Green
- Ladder Golf
- Beanbag Toss

Skateboard Ramp

Because good places to practice can be few and far between, every skateboarder dreams of having a skateboard ramp of his or her own. Sidewalks may get dull, city streets are dangerous, and most public areas are rarely skateboarder-friendly; but your own ramp in your own yard is always ready and available.

This skateboard ramp (knowledgeable boarders would describe it as a mini half-pipe ramp) is a fun, challenging, and safe place to learn new skills—and it offers a softer landing than a hard concrete sidewalk. It's also fun to build and can be constructed in two to four days using only standard hand and power tools.

This 4-foot-high ramp measures 24 feet long by eight feet wide. It is built in three sections: a pair of curved ramps on each end and a flat stretch in between. To keep the plywood that forms the curves from wicking up moisture and rotting, build it on top of concrete footings or pads. If you build it on a flat driveway or patio, set the corners and center transitions on concrete pads to keep the wood dry.

Skateboarding is a dangerous activity on ramps or anywhere else. Always wear a helmet, kneepads, and other protective clothing and equipment when skateboarding. *Note: This ramp is based on a free plan designed by Rick Dahlen and available for downloading. See Resources, page 236.*

Materials ▸

¾" exterior plywood	Lag screws (⅜ × 3")
⅜" exterior plywood (sanded)	with washers
2 × 4 lumber (pressure-treated)	Carriage bolts (⅜ × 4") with washers and nuts
2 × 4 lumber (no. 2 or better)	#6 panhead screws (1½")
Deck screws (1⅝, 2, 2½")	Schedule 40 PVC tubing (2" dia.)

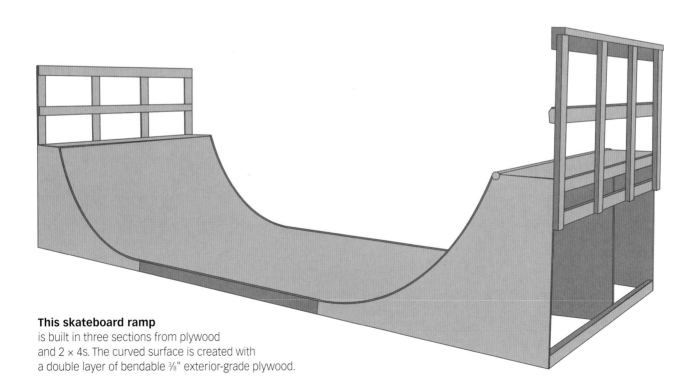

This skateboard ramp
is built in three sections from plywood
and 2 × 4s. The curved surface is created with
a double layer of bendable ⅜" exterior-grade plywood.

How to Build a Skateboard Ramp

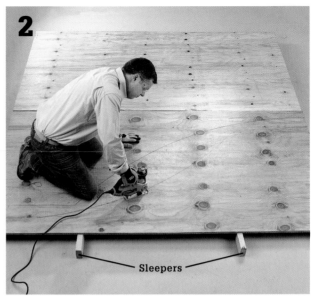

Mark the curves for the ramp sides using a modified trammel. First, lay two sheets of ¾"-thick exterior plywood next to each other on a flat surface. The long edges should be touching, with the ends flush. Cut a thin strip of wood to 8-ft. long and tack one end 3½" up from one of the back ends. Measure 7 ft.-6" from the point where the trammel strip is tacked and drill a ⅜"-dia. guide hole for a pencil. Insert a pencil into the guide hole and trace a curve on the plywood. Mark four pieces of plywood this way.

Cut out the curves using a jigsaw equipped with a fast wood-cutting blade. Watch the lines carefully as you cut to avoid drifting away from the curve, and make sure both the workpiece and the waste are well supported. Setting the plywood on 2 × 4 sleepers creates access space for the jigsaw blade.

Cut notches for the coping pipe at the top of each curved plywood upright, using a jigsaw. The notches allow the PVC coping pipe that is used to overhang the ramp slightly.

Build the ramp side assemblies. Cut the 2 × 4 spreaders to length using a power miter saw equipped with a stop block for uniform lengths. Install the spreaders between pairs of ramp sides at intervals of approximately 8". Drive several 2½" deck screws through the plywood and into the ends of the spreaders at each joint.

5

Bevel the top spreaders. Two spreaders are butted together at the top of each ramp to create a cradle for the coping tube (here, a piece of 2" PVC pipe). Butt a spreader up against the face of the top spreader in each ramp and mark a bevel cut on the edge so you can trim the spreader to be flush with the plywood base. Rip the bevel cut on a table saw or clamp the workpiece securely to a support board and cut the bevel with a straightedge guide and a circular saw. Set the saw blade angle to match the bevel angle.

6

Construct the 2 × 4 platform for the flat middle area in two sections and then fasten the sections together with deck screws. Alternate driving directions between frames to create a stronger joint.

7

Join all the curved and flat sections with deck screws, aligning the edges carefully. By this time, you should have moved the parts to the installation area and confirmed that the area is flat. Ideally, the ramp should be installed on a concrete slab or concrete footings that minimize ground contact.

8

Coping tube shown cutaway for clarity

Add the coping tube to the tops of the ramps—we used 2"-dia. Schedule 40 PVC tubing, but you can use rigid conduit or water pipe if you prefer metal. Drill eight evenly spaced $3/16$" holes through the coping, then enlarge the entry holes to $1/2$". Fasten the coping to the beveled top spreaders with $1 1/2$", #6 panhead screws.

(continued)

Install a layer of ¾" plywood to the flat areas of the ramp using 2" deck screws driven every 8" into the platform frames. Choose exterior-rated plywood with a sanded face facing upward to create a smooth skateboarding surface. Make sure joints between panels fall over 2 × 4 supports and make sure all screw heads are recessed slightly below the wood surface.

Attach a double layer of ⅜" plywood to the curved parts of the ramp. Standard ¾" plywood is too thick to bend along the ramp curves, so we used two layers of ⅜" plywood, which is limber enough to manage the gradual curves of the ramp. Make sure the seams for both layers are offset by at least 18" and that all joints fall over 2 × 4s. Leave ⅛" gaps between sheets for expansion and drainage. Attach with 1⅝" deck screws driven every 8". *Tip: To help the plywood bend more easily, dampen the reverse side.*

11

At the joint between the coping and the deck, spread a bead of caulk along the top edge of the first layer to keep water from wicking in between the sheets and rotting the wood. Caulk the gap between the coping tube and the first course before you butt the second course of plywood up to the coping. Fasten the plywood with 2" deck screws. *Tip: For a better joint, bevel-rip the top edge of the second course slightly.*

12

Bolt 2 × 4" × 4-ft. posts to the back of each platform using ⅜ × 4" carriage bolts. Attach an additional 2 × 4" × 4-ft. corner post at each side to create L-shaped corners. Draw the corner post boards together with 2½" deck screws, closing the joint.

13

Install horizontal rails between the posts and then top-off each end rail system with a 2 × 4 cap plate attached with 2½" deck screws.

14

Sand the plywood to eliminate roughness and splinters, and set any protruding screws beneath the surface of the plywood. Vacuum the dust off, then coat all wood with paint or wood preservative. For best protection and ease of cleaning, coat the entire ramp with two or three thin coats of gloss exterior paint.

Basketball Hoop

Basketball is one of the few sports where you can have as much fun competing against yourself as you can competing with others. If you have kids (or even if you don't) a basketball hoop in the driveway or backyard is an excellent investment.

A huge range of basketball hoops are available. Which one to select depends on your needs, your budget, and your yard or driveway. A hoop can be as simple as a metal rim screwed to the side of a garage or as elaborate as a heavy-duty, professional-quality system supported by a 48-inch-deep concrete base with six-foot-wide tempered glass backboard (not to mention a professionally-installed court with permanent markings). Within this range, the main choices are a portable goal (a pole and backboard supported by a wide, heavy base on wheels); a wall-mounted or roof-mounted backboard and goal; or a freestanding post set in concrete, with backboard and rim attached. You can buy any of these types with the basket and backboard fixed in place, or you can choose a goal that has an adjustable height feature—a good option if you have small children.

Whether you're shooting hoops alone and working on your skills, or playing organized games with a group of friends, basketball is an absorbing, exciting game that never gets boring and is great exercise.

Basketball Goals

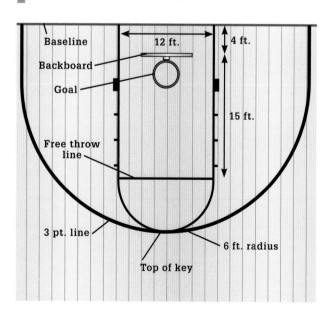

Court Layout. For a regulation half-court game (or full-court, if you have the space), tape off and paint your own home court or buy a stencil kit from a sports supply store.

A backboard is easy and fun to make from ¾" exterior grade plywood. Cut the shape with a jigsaw and seal all cut edges with wood preservative before priming and painting white. Use paint or tape to create the black outlines and the orange target box.

Freestanding Goals

A traditional basketball post is set in concrete. This works well when you have a dedicated space for the court, as shown here.

Wall-mounted Goals

Wall-mounted goals can be attached directly to the gable area of a garage or secured by angled support arms that are attached to a low-slope roof.

Direct-mounted Goals

48"-deep footing

Heavier backboards and posts require a more substantial concrete base. The welded base plate is bolted to large J-bolts buried in the reinforced concrete base. Adjust the nuts underneath the plate to make the pole perfectly plumb. The concrete base is 48" deep (minimum) and 16" or more in diameter, with metal rebar inserted to help anchor the J-bolts. This type of post set-up is typically expensive.

A glass goal is bolted directly to support arms that are attached to the post. In many cases the goal can be lowered from the standard 10-ft. height if you have smaller children.

Bocce Court

Like many sports and games, bocce can be played casually on any reasonably level lawn with a minimum of rules, depending on how flexible you and your playing companions are. But if you are serious about playing bocce as a pastime and you have the space in your yard, consider building a regulation bocce court with a smooth, flat surface and a permanent border.

Developed in Italy as a variation of an ancient Roman game and then spread around the world, bocce is played at clubs, public courts, and backyards all over the world. Although not an Olympic sport, various bocce federations and clubs organize tournaments for enthusiastic amateurs, and competition can be fierce.

Official bocce courts for tournament play are 13 feet wide by 91 feet long, but recreational courts can be anywhere from 8 to 14 feet wide and 60 to 91 feet long. If you're trying to squeeze a court into your backyard, you can adjust those measurements as needed. Often the game is played without a court at all, or with an irregular-shaped court that accommodates the dimensions and shape of your yard. Standard courts are made from gravel topped with a fine clay or shell mixture and surrounded by a low wood wall, with the depth and composition of gravel and the construction of the wood wall determined by local climate and soil conditions.

Borders should be made of wood, and can be constructed of 4 × 4s, 4 × 6s, 2 × 10s, or other combinations of sizes. No matter which size you use, the border should be protected from frost heave and moisture, either by anchoring it to 4 × 6 posts set in concrete below the frost line or by building it on a thick bed of gravel.

Large, pressure-treated timbers like 6 × 6s and 6 × 8s make an excellent border, but these can be difficult to work with unless you're using a bobcat. You can substitute built-up layers of 2× lumber and 4 × 4s instead, overlapping seams and nailing and bolting them together. Bolt or screw them together from the outside, so that there are no visible fasteners on the inside of the court.

Bocce is a popular backyard game that has been around for centuries. It can be played free-form in any backyard, but for the truly authentic bocce experience you'll want a hard-surface bocce court.

Tools & Materials ▸

4 × 6 pressure-treated timbers	Circular saw
2 × 10 pressure-treated timbers	Concrete mix
1½ to 2"-dia. drainage rock	Drill and spade bits
Compactable gravel	Laser level
Tennis court clay, crushed oyster shells or similar blend	Stakes
	Mason's string
	Flat nose spade
Lag bolts, washers, and nuts	Shovel
	Trowel
2½" deck screws	Power tamper
Construction adhesive	Construction adhesive
Posthole digger	Eye and ear protection
Gravel compactor	Work gloves

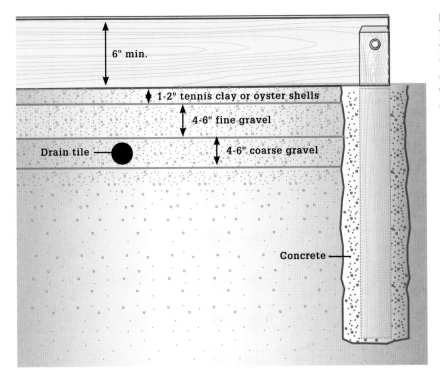

6" min.

1-2" tennis clay or oyster shells

4-6" fine gravel

Drain tile ●

4-6" coarse gravel

Concrete

Frame the court with wood planks or timbers supported by frost footings or a thick gravel pad. Build the court surface from coarse gravel topped with finer, crushed limestone or similar stone, topped with crushed oyster shells, tennis clay or other similar material.

How to Play Bocce ▶

Bocce is played between two players or two teams of up to four players each. Eight large balls and one small ball called a "pallino" are used. The pallino is thrown out first. The object of the game is to get one of the large balls as close as possible to the pallino. Knocking the other team's balls away from the pallino is acceptable. For a much more in-depth version of the rules, along with playing strategies and penalties, visit www.boccestandardsassociation.org and the United States Bocce Federation at www.bocce.com.

Composite

Clay

Pallino

Bocce is played with a set of eight bocce balls and one target ball. Introductory sets made from composites can be purchased for less than $50. A traditional set of bocce balls made from clay and imported from Italy costs considerably more, but is a near-necessity if you develop a serious attachment to the game.

How to Build a Bocce Court

Find or create a level area in your yard and stake out the corners of the bocce court. See previous page for discussion of court dimensions. Strip back the sod from the court area with a sod cutter or a flat nose spade.

Excavate the topsoil in the court area. A regulation bocce court should be dug out a minimum of 10" so the proper subbase material can be put in. If your plans are more casual, you can cheat this step a little as long as the ground in your yard is not soft enough that the court will sink.

Dig postholes. To support the walls (and prevent them from moving) set pressure-treated 4 × 6 landscape timbers every 4 ft. around the perimeter of the court. Ideally, the timbers (installed vertically) should extend past the frostline for your area. The tops will be trimmed to about 6" above grade after they're set.

Set the 4 × 6 timbers into the post holes, with a 4 to 6" layer of drainage gravel at the bottom. Fill around the timbers with concrete, sloping the tops to shed water. After all of the posts are set and the concrete is dry, use a laser level to mark level cutting lines on all the post tops and then trim them to height with a circular saw or reciprocating saw.

Option: After cutting the posts to height, use a circular saw set at 45°, a planer, or a trim router with a chamfer bit to cut chamfer profiles into the tops of the posts. Cut the outer edge and side edges of each post. Do not cut a chamfer on the side that will butt against the court walls.

Spread a 4 to 6" layer of drainage rock, such as 1½" river rock, onto the court. Cover this with a 4 to 6" layer of compactable gravel and tamp the gravel thoroughly with a power tamper. Add more gravel and tamp until you have attained a very firm base that is at or slightly below ground level.

Build the walls. Lay pressure-treated 2 × 10 lumber around the perimeter inside the posts. This first layer of the wall should be laid on edge, with the end seams falling at post locations. Fasten the boards to the posts with counterbored lag bolts, washers, and nuts. Then, attach a second layer of 2 × 10 inside the first layer. Use heavy duty construction adhesive and 2½" deck screws driven through the outer layer and into the inner layer.

Add a 1 to 2"-thick top layer of court clay, crushed oyster shells or other suitable medium. Here, crushed stone is being raked in preparation for compaction. Some top-dress layers do not require tamping, as the material will settle naturally. If the surface remains loose, however, you can use a power compactor to harden the surface so the bocce balls will roll more easily.

Batting Cage

Baseball is great fun, but it's a tough game to play by oneself. For a serious player—or for anyone who simply enjoys hitting a ball around—a batting cage ranges anywhere from a luxury to a necessity. Made of netting hung from a steel frame, a batting cage allows you to hit balls in any direction, as hard as you can, without having to waste hours chasing them down (or putting every window in your neighborhood at risk).

Naturally, a batting cage requires some way to deliver a pitched ball. A live pitcher (Hi, Dad) with an L-shaped screen protector can be used. Or, you can purchase a pitching machine. For home use, pitching machines can be purchased for as little as $100, but for a decent tool that won't frustrate you completely, expect to spend at least $350—and probably more.

Batting cages are freestanding, with angled frames that can be assembled in a few hours. Lengths of steel tubing are inserted into 3- or 4-way fittings and assembled into a tentlike frame, then the netting is hung on the frame and attached to the poles. Stakes and ropes are used to hold the cage in place, though the consumer-grade cages are not designed to stay up year-round in winter, or even to survive severe weather.

Larger, more expensive models of batting cages have support tubes in sleeves that are set into concrete footings, allowing you to remove the cage and tubes for the winter. Heavy-duty types used by colleges and professional teams employ heavy steel posts set permanently into deep footings and can cost several thousands of dollars.

Although netting can be purchased separately from Internet suppliers, it is difficult to imagine a situation where constructing your own batting cage from wood or even PVC tubing and then having the netting custom sewn would have any advantage. A flat area, an extension cord and a batting cage kit are the best ingredients to creating your own backyard batting cage.

Pitchbacks ▸

To complement your batting cage, get an inexpensive pitchback so you can practice pitching and fielding. Most types will also work with soccer or basketballs and can be adjusted to bounce balls back in different ways.

Sharpen your hitting skills without wasting all your time retrieving the ball. With a batting cage and a pitching machine—or a willing friend—you can hit balls all day long.

Golf Net

Golf nets work on the same principle as batting cages, but because a golf ball is so much smaller than a baseball or softball, they use a smaller mesh net and have a different design. Unlike batting practice, you usually don't need to worry about hitting golf balls straight up into the air or having them skitter away directly behind you when you swing and miss. Usually.

Larger golf nets are sold as kits similar to batting cage kits. There is some basic work involved in assembling them: you have to erect the metal frame and attach the netting. In fact, larger golf nets are often made and sold by the same manufacturers as batting cages, and some even can be set up inside the batting cage (the mesh is half the diameter). Many types have a center target that makes a distinctive sound when you hit it so you can tell if you are aiming your drives correctly.

Smaller golf nets resemble pop-up tents or play tunnels more than semipermanent cages that live in your yard (at least during golf season). These small cages are available online and at golf or sporting equipment stores.

Golf netting is also available by the square foot from Internet suppliers. It is possible to build your own cage by hanging the netting from a homemade support frame, and you can probably save a few dollars by approaching it that way. But using a professionally designed and built model is always a better recommendation.

Work on your swing all day long with a golf net. The center target helps you learn to hold your club correctly and hit the ball properly.

Horseshoe Pit

Horseshoes and a similar game called quoits—which is played with rings instead of horseshoes—both evolved out of games played by soldiers in ancient Greece and Rome. In the US, horseshoes was popular in both the Revolutionary and Civil War. Returning soldiers brought it back with them to their towns and farms, where it quickly took root, largely because most households already had all the equipment needed to play it—a few unattached horseshoes and two metal stakes.

According to the National Horseshoe Pitchers Association, regulation court size is 48 feet from end to end, with 40 feet in between goal stakes. Stakes are made of one-inch-diameter steel 36 inches in length, and angle toward one another at 12 degrees. From 14 to 15 inches of post should protrude above ground. Horseshoes must not weigh more than three pounds. The ideal surface for the "pit" that cushions the horseshoes when they land and stops them from kicking up clods of dirt is moist blue clay, but sand or even loose dirt are acceptable.

Horseshoes are pitched from behind a foul line 37 feet away from the opposite stake, but the official rules allow women, children under 18, and men over 70 to pitch their horseshoes from 27 feet away from the opposite stake, if they so desire.

Rules for Horseshoes ▶

Stand by the stake at one end of the court and throw the horseshoe to the other end. If your horseshoe rings the stake (a ringer), you get three points. If no one gets a ringer, you get one point if your horseshoe is right next to the stake. Each player gets two horseshoes, and the first player to get 21 points wins.

Horseshoes has been played for thousands of years, and is an easy game to set up in the back or side yard. A permanent horseshoe pit is a fun, easy project to build.

Creating a Horseshoe Pit

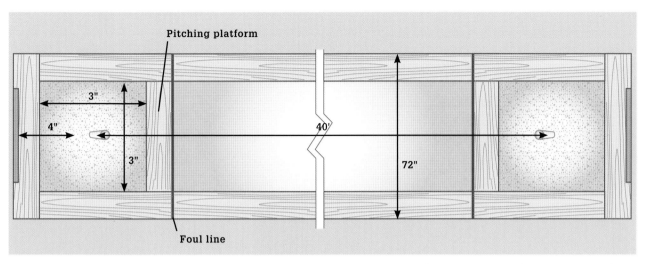

A typical horseshoes court. The most important dimension to know for horseshoes is that you need 40 ft. between the stakes. Other lines can be added with lime or other sport field marker as you become more serious about the game.

A regulation horseshoe pit is a 3-ft. square with 4" of loose sand on top. The stake is a 1" steel rod or pipe sticking 14" out of the ground and angled away from the backstop at 12°. The backstops (optional but a very good idea) are made from pressure-treated 2 × 8 lumber attached to 2 × 4 stakes drive into the ground. They are 4 ft. from the stake. Inset: An integral backstop and side arms form a cozy pit that keeps horseshoes under control, even if it doesn't quite meet the official regulations.

Multi-use Sports Court

Sports courts are a great way to get a professional-quality playing surface in your backyard. Usually professionally installed, they are made from 9/16-inch-thick interlocking plastic tiles that have tightly spaced grids to allow water to flow through. The tiles come in different colors and can be painted with different court lines, allowing you to play several different games on one court (but not all at the same time). Multi-use sports courts are generally built with a basketball hoop and a pole or poles that can be used for net games. Posts and poles for tetherball, batting cages, street hockey, and other games can be integrated into the court.

The sport-court tiles are laid onto a four-inch-thick concrete slab on a gravel base (depending on local climate). The slab should be sloped slightly so that water can run off. The concrete surface also should be broomed lightly before the concrete sets to give it a texture that the tiles can grip. The tiles are not affixed directly to the concrete, so they can move easily with temperature changes. They are securely held in place by their weight and the friction of the concrete, however, so slippage during competition is not a problem. Single tiles can be pried out easily for replacement. Tiles are cut with utility knives.

Although generally installed by specialty contractors, the tiles can be purchased and installed by homeowners. The most technically demanding part of the installation is the concrete slab—once that and the footings for the basketball hoop and other poles are in place, installing the tiles is straightforward. The court seen here was installed by Sport Court North (see Resources, page 236).

Tools & Materials ▸

Gravel	Tape dispenser
Concrete	Earth-moving equipment
Concrete tools	Posts for basketball,
Netting	volleyball, etc.
Laser level	Sports court interlocking
Work gloves	tiles
Paint	Eye and ear protection
Foam roller	

With a multi-use sports court surface you can have a professional-quality sports surface that can be used for a variety of sports in your backyard, including basketball, volleyball, badminton, pickleball and tennis.

Multi-use Sport-court Installation

Sport-court tile grids are laid onto a concrete slab to create a nonslip surface that's easy to keep clean. Double-check to make sure your slab is square first, and then install the interlocking tiles beginning in one corner.

Create a free throw lane for a basketball court or service courts for tennis by switching to a different color tile. Tiles are available in a variety of colors, allowing you to create different areas within any court. The tiles interlock with pegs and loops and are open so water drains through (inset).

Pivot pole

To center

Tape dispenser

Use tape to create sharp, crisp edges for painted court lines. The tape dispenser here is pivoting on a long pole anchored to a centerpoint at the top of the key in the free throw lane. You can make a homemade version of this curving tape dispenser with lengths of plastic pipe and pipe fittings.

Paint between the lines with a foam roller, first with primer, then with a topcoat. Use special paints recommended by the tile manufacturer or a paint dealer.

Tetherball

A favorite at summer camps, tetherball is a simple but vigorous game for two people that involves hitting a ball on a rope back and forth around a pole until one player manages to wrap the ball completely around the pole. There is no governing body and little in the way of formal competition, but a basic set of rules has evolved to make the game fair and competitive, because otherwise a server who knows how to hit the ball will win every time.

Kits with metal poles and balls are available, but you can save money and get a sturdier pole if you make your own from galvanized pipe and then buy the ball with attached rope separately. The pole must be long enough to extend 10 feet above ground level, and the ball should hang two feet above the ground. To make a strong, removable pole, set a two-foot length of pipe with a threaded coupling in a concrete base; then thread the 10-foot pole with an eyebolt at the top into the coupling.

Tetherballs with rope attached are available at sporting goods stores and on the Internet. Unless you're an experienced player, buy the soft version of the ball—it's easier on kids' hands.

Tetherball Rules ▶

Number of players: Two

The serve: Players stand on opposite sides of a 20-foot-diameter circle. The server begins play by hitting the ball around the pole in one direction. The opponent hits the ball around the pole in the other direction. The first player to wrap the rope completely around the pole is the winner.

Fouls: If a player commits a foul (see below), play stops and the player making the foul must give up his turn.

1. Hitting the ball twice at the serve before the opponent hits the ball
2. Hitting the tetherball with a part of the body other than one's hand or forearm
3. Holding, catching, or throwing the ball while play is ongoing
4. Stepping over the centerline
5. Reaching around the pole to hit the ball
6. Hitting the ball twice on your side of the court
7. Touching the pole
8. Hitting or touching the rope

Tetherball is a fast-moving game with plenty of hitting and jumping that fits easily into a small backyard.

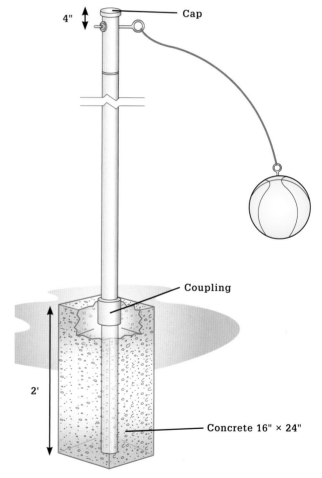

Dig a 2 ft. × 16" hole, set the assembled pole in the center, and plumb it in both directions with wood braces. Fill the hole with concrete to just below the top of the coupling, then slope the concrete to the outside so water doesn't pool around the pipe. Use plenty of pipe thread compound when you assemble the sections of pipe to protect the threads from rust and make it easier to remove the pole if it becomes necessary. Tighten the pipe with a pipe wrench so it doesn't loosen during play.

Pickleball

Pickleball is a relative newcomer to the world of backyard games. With elements of tennis, badminton, and ping pong, it is played on a court roughly half the size of a tennis court (identical to a doubles badminton court) using paddles and a lightweight plastic ball. Despite the name, pickles are neither used nor consumed during play—the game was named in honor of the family dog of one of the co-inventors of the sport.

The pickleball court is 20 feet wide—the same width as a two-car driveway—and can be played on asphalt, concrete, wood, clay, or plastic-tiled sports courts. The USA Pickleball Association organizes tournaments and sells an official rulebook, though the basic game is simple to learn (see Resources, page 236).

Pickleball is played with wood or graphite paddles, hollow plastic balls and a net (a badminton net will work).

Pickleball Rules ▶

The game starts with a serve (always underhand) from the right court to the right court on the other side, like tennis. On the first serve the ball must bounce once before the opposing team can return it, then bounce once before the serving team hits it back. After those two bounces it can be returned in the air or after bouncing once. You can only score when serving, and you score when the other team has a fault, such as missing the ball, hitting it into the net or knocking it out of bounds. If the serving team faults, the other team serves. The first team to reach 11 with a two-point margin wins.

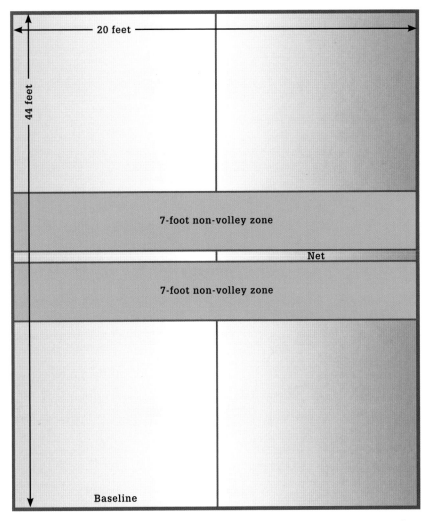

20 feet

44 feet

7-foot non-volley zone

Net

7-foot non-volley zone

Baseline

The official pickleball court size is 20 ft. wide and 44 ft. long, with a 7 ft. no-volley zone by the net. The net is 36" high at the sides and 34" high in the center.

Putting Green

Serious golfers often say they "drive for show and putt for dough," and most of them practice putting at every opportunity. For these folks, a backyard putting green is the very definition of luxury.

Natural grass putting greens offer the ultimate in luxurious golf environments at home, but they require special breeds of grass and very specialized maintenance that very few people have the time or equipment to provide. But if you are willing to forego the smell of the fresh-cut Bermuda grass and the feel of a well-tended green underfoot, you'll find that there are a number of artificial putting green options that offer a chance to hone your putting stroke.

The panels and turf we used for making a putting green can be purchased on the Internet. The systems are easy to install and produces a good practice surface—a fine combination when it comes to putting greens.

Tools & Materials ▸

Line trimmer	Hammer	Garden hose or rope	Chalk
Heavy scissors	Graph paper	Spray paint	Straightedge
Screwdriver	Putting green panels	Sand	Rake
Jigsaw	Artificial turf	Landscape fabric	Eye and ear protection
Spade	Turf spikes	Fabric staples	Work gloves
Utility knife	Turf tape		

Backyard putting greens give golfers a whole new way to have fun and perfect their game. Special kits, including panels and artificial turf, make building one an easy weekend project.

Designing a Backyard Putting Green

Choose an above-ground green for seasonal use or even to use indoors. They lack a bit of authenticity, but they are very convenient.

Kit accessories, such as pins and edge liners, give a backyard putting green a more genuine flavor. A chipping mat can be positioned around the green to let you work on your close-in short game without destroying your yard.

Artificial turf comes in an array of styles and lengths. Lower nap products, like the two samples to the left, are best for putting greens.

How to Install a Backyard Putting Green

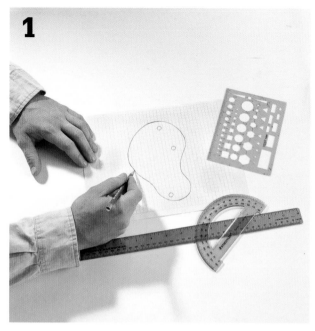

Diagram your putting green on graph paper, including cup locations. If you are ordering your kit from an Internet seller, they probably have a mapping and planning program on their website. Order panels and turf as necessary to create your putting green.

As soon as it arrives, unroll the turf and spray it with water to saturate. Set the turf aside and let it dry for at least 24 hours. This process preshrinks the turf.

Measure the installation area and mark the perimeter of the putting green, using a garden hose or rope. Lift the hose or rope and spray-paint the green's outline onto the grass. Some putting green kits are precut to create specific shapes and sizes, while others offer a bit more design flexibility.

Inside the outlined area, use a line trimmer to scalp the grass down to the dirt. Rake up and remove any debris.

Add sand or remove dirt as necessary to create contours in the putting green. Kit manufacturers suggest that you create the contours that replicate the breaks you most want to practice. For example, if you have trouble hitting uphill and to the right, create a hill and place the cup at the top and to the right.

Cover the scalped and contoured installation area with landscape fabric, overlapping seams by at least 2". Trim the fabric to fit inside the outline and secure it to the ground with landscape fabric staples.

Starting in the center of the installation area, push two panels together and hold them tightly in place as you insert the fasteners. Use a screwdriver to tighten the fasteners. Install the panels in locations indicated on your diagram.

Continue to fill in panels, according to your plan. Take special notice of putting cup locations. In many kits, these require special panels with cups preinstalled. Locate them according to your plan.

(continued)

Where panels go beyond the outline, use a light-colored crayon or chalk to mark a cutting line. Avoid cutting into the interlocking panel edges.

One panel at a time, cut panels to shape, using a jigsaw with a blade that's slightly longer than the panel thickness. Use panel scraps to fill in open areas in the layout wherever you can, and then mark and cut the scraps to fit.

Dig a 4"-wide by 4"-deep trench around the perimeter of the green shape, directly next to the edge of the panels.

Place the artificial turf on top of the panels. Pay attention to the nap of the turf to make sure it all runs in the same direction. Use a utility knife to cut it to size, 4" larger than the panel assembly.

Install the cups into the panels containing the cup bodies, and then cut holes in the turf with a utility knife.

Fold back the edges of the turf. Apply double-sided carpet tape to the perimeter of the panel assembly. Peel off the tape's protective cover, then press the turf down onto the tape. Fold the excess turf over the edge of the panel assembly and down into the trench. If the turf bulges around a tight radius, make 3½" slashes in the edge of the turf and ease it around the curve.

Drive carpet spikes or fabric spikes (provided by the kit manufacturer) through the edges of the turf and into the trench to secure the turf.

Backfill the trench with the soil you removed earlier. Add landscaping around the edges of the green, if desired. Sweep and hose down the green periodically and as needed.

Ladder Golf

adder golf doesn't have much to do with golf, but it's plenty of fun and it's exploding in popularity. Stop by any tailgate party outside the football stadium and there's a good chance you'll see several fans engaged in a heated game. Also called ladder toss, ladder ball, and many other names (some not especially polite), ladder golf is a relatively new backyard game that involves tossing short bolas made from golf balls at a ladderlike stand. If the bola wraps around one of the ladder rungs and stays, you earn points. You can make your own ladder golf game in a few hours using PVC tubing, some ⅜" nylon rope, and a dozen golf balls in two different colors. It's best to make a pair of goals so all the players don't have to traipse back and forth after every turn, but a single goal is adequate to play.

Tools & Materials ▸

(3) ¾" × 10' CPVC	⅜"-dia. × 20' nylon rope	Drill press and ⅜" bit	Ear protection
(6) ¾" CPVC T-fittings	(12) Solid-core golf balls	Sand	Safety glasses
(6) ¾" CPVC elbows	Hand screw (wood clamp)	Electrical tape	Work gloves
PVC primer and cement	Tubing cutter		

Ladder golf is a fun (some would say addictive) backyard game that anyone can play. The goals and the golf ball bolas are easy and cheap to make yourself.

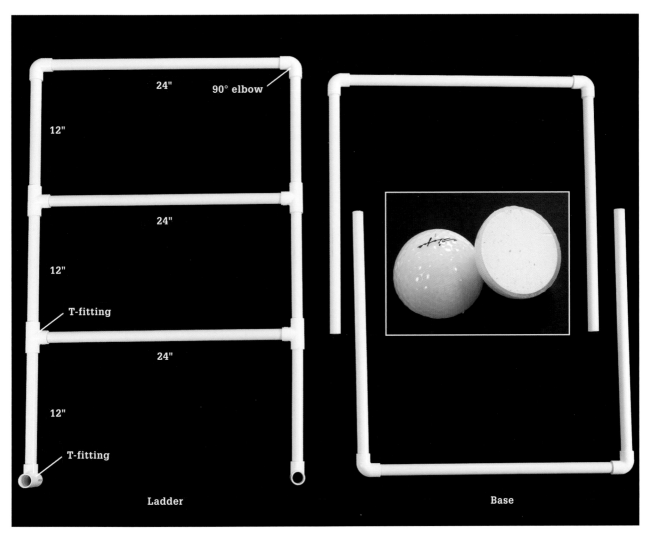

24"	90° elbow
12"	
24"	
12"	
T-fitting	
24"	
12"	
T-fitting	

Ladder   **Base**

Ordinary PVC tubing is used to make the goals for ladder golf. You'll need six 12" lengths and nine 24" lengths, along with six tee fittings, sand, and six elbow fittings. Inset: Look for solid-core golf balls. Top-Flite is one common brand name that has a solid core. Balls with liquid or gel cores will leak unpleasant chemicals if you drill through the middle.

Ladder Golf Rules ▸

Ladder golf can be played by any number of players or teams, with each player using three bolas. The top rung of the ladder is worth three points, the middle is two points, and the bottom is one point. The official throwing line is 15 feet from the ladder, but children and the elderly may play closer. Each player throws all three of their bolas before the next player has a turn, and the player who has exactly 21 points at the end of a round of play wins.

Players are allowed to:
- Throw the bola in any way they wish, including bouncing.
- Knock other players' bolas off the ladder, thus taking away their points.

- Distract opponents with questions, loud remarks and rude noises.

Players are not allowed to:
- Touch or hit opposing players, even gently.

If a player goes over 21 points in a round, none of that player's points for that round count. A player who wraps all three bolas around the same step or around each of the three steps during one round of play earns one extra point.

If more than one player gets 21 points, the tying players continue playing rounds until one of them finishes two points ahead of the other.

How to Make Ladder Golf Goals

Cut all of the parts for each goal to length from ¾" CPVC tubing. If you have one, use a tubing cutter for clean cut. You can use a hacksaw instead and deburr the cut ends with emery paper.

Test fit the parts to dry-assemble each goal. In most cases, the fit between tubing and fittings is tight enough that a simple friction fit with no glue will hold the parts together. This has the added benefit of letting you disassemble the goal easily.

Permanent Connections ▶

Solvent-glue the parts together for a permanent goal that will not fall apart during use. PVC primer alone will create a strong enough bond that the parts are unlikely to come apart, but if you foresee great stress you can use solvent glue. One compromise option to gluing versus not gluing is to glue the parts of the upright together and to glue the parts of the feet together, but allow the joints where the uprights meet the feet to be friction-fit only. That way, the parts can be partially disassembled for easy storage and transport.

Wrap bands of narrow electrical tape (comes in multiple colors) around the scoring bars as a scoring reminder.

How to Make Ladder Golf Bolas

Secure a solid-core golf ball (See page 125) into the jaws of a wooden handscrew clamp. It is very important that the ball be secured during drilling.

Set the handscrew clamp with the golf ball onto the table of a drill press and position it so the ball is centered under the point of a ⅜" bit. Drill all the way through the ball. You can use a drill without a drill press, but take great care and make sure the clamp is well secured to the worksurface.

Feed ⅜" nylon rope through the hole in a golf ball. Tie one end tightly to secure the golf ball, and then feed the other end through another golf ball. Tie that end so the distance between golf balls is 13".

Trim the ends of the ropes so about ½" sticks out from each knot. Carefully singe the nylon fibers so they melt together and will not unravel.

Beanbag Toss

Beanbag toss was invented, by most accounts, during the darkness of the middle ages in Europe. Lost for centuries, it was rediscovered in the back woods of Kentucky in the 19th century. However, the basic idea of the game—throw something at a target—has existed uninterrupted for many thousands of years.

Little equipment is needed to play beanbag toss—just a pair of wooden boxes with holes and several small cloth bags filled with dried beans or corn. The object is to throw the beanbags into the holes. The two boxes are placed so that the holes are 33 feet apart for standard play, though you may move the targets closer for players with limited throwing range. Players stand to the side of a box when pitching. Each player gets four bags to throw. A bag that goes into the hole is worth three points, a bag that lands on the box and stays put is worth one point, and a bag that ends up off the box is worth nothing. The first player to 21 wins.

Tools & Materials ▸

½ sheet (4 × 4')	Jigsaw
¼" plywood	Drill/driver
2 × 4s	Duck cloth (for bags)
2½" deck screws	Dry Navy beans for bags
Panel adhesive	Needle and thread or
4d finish nails	sewing machine
Exterior wood primer	Sandpaper
Exterior paint	Eye and ear protection
Circular saw	Work gloves

Making Beanbags ▸

You can purchase beanbags inexpensively at any toy store, or you can make your own using dry navy beans or unpopped popcorn and extra cloth. Make bags in sets of four, each from matching cloth. You'll need four bags per player. (Two to four players is typical). To make each bag, sew two 7" square pieces of duck cloth together on three sides, turn it inside out, and fill with two cups of dry beans or feed corn (it should be about 14 to 16oz.). Tuck the open end into the bag, pin it and then sew it shut and stitch around all the edges. The finished bag should be approximately 6 × 6".

Despite its simplicity, a serious game of beanbag toss can last for hours. Dried beans are the usual filler for the bags, though dried corn is preferred in some areas of the country.

How to Make a Beanbag Toss Game

Cut the plywood underlayment panel into 24 × 48" boards using a circular saw and straightedge cutting guide (or a tablesaw if you have one). Lay out a 6"-dia. hole 6" down from the top of each panel and cut it out using a jigsaw. *Tip: Jigsaws cut on the upstroke, so cut from the underside of the panel (if it has one) to minimize tear out on the top. Sand the cut edges thoroughly to smooth the edges and remove splinters.*

Assemble the frame. Drive 2½" decks screws at the corner joints, making sure the corners are square. Cut two 11½" long lengths of 2 × 4 for the legs for each target. Attach the legs by driving 2½" deck screws through the legs and into the inside of the target frame. Attach the top panel to the frame with panel adhesive and 4d finish nails.

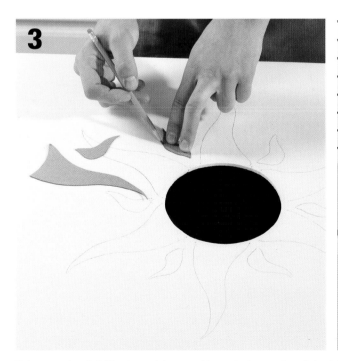

Prime and paint the target boxes. Use exterior-grade paints. Add creative designs with acrylic hobby paints.. Select a fun pattern, such as the sunrays seen here.

Projects for Backyard Entertaining

Backyard recreation isn't just for kids, and it involves much more than running and climbing. For adults, there's the enduring appeal of activities like grilling a meal outdoors, watching a crackling fire as the sun goes down, or just sitting on a deck chair observing birds as they visit the environment you've created to attract them. These may be small, bucolic pleasures that lack the aerobic excitement of intense physical activity, but they help to keep us whole.

This section focuses mostly on projects that extend the comforts of the living area to the outside of the house, creating new places to entertain or to unwind after a long day of work. You'll find projects designed to make you a more popular host to friends and family (or to wildlife), but you'll also find projects that offer entertainment benefits even if your idea of entertaining is on the solitary side.

In this chapter:

- Outdoor Kitchen
- Outdoor Kitchen Walls
  & Countertop
- Firepit
- Backyard Theater
- Wildlife Observation

Outdoor Kitchen

With its perfect blend of indoor convenience and alfresco atmosphere, it's easy to see why the outdoor kitchen is one of today's most popular home upgrades. In terms of design, outdoor kitchens can take almost any form, but most are planned around the essential elements of a built-in grill and convenient countertop surfaces (preferably on both sides of the grill). Secure storage inside the cooking cabinet is another feature many outdoor cooks find indispensable.

The kitchen design in this project combines all three of these elements in a moderately-sized cooking station that can fit a variety of kitchen configurations.

The structure is freestanding and self-supporting, so it can go almost anywhere—on top of a patio, right next to a house wall, out by the pool, or out in the yard to create a remote entertainment getaway. Adding a table and chairs or a casual sitting area might be all you need to complete your kitchen accommodations. But best of all, this kitchen is made almost entirely of inexpensive masonry materials.

Concrete and masonry are ideally suited to outdoor kitchen construction. Both are noncombustible, not damaged by water, and can easily withstand decades of outdoor exposure. In fact, a little weathering makes masonry look even better. In this project, the kitchen's structural cabinet is built with concrete block on top of a reinforced concrete slab. The countertop is two-inch-thick poured concrete that you cast in place over two layers of cementboard.

Tools & Materials ▸

Chalk line	Straightedge	Steel angle iron	Finish coat stucco
Pointing trowel	Square-notched trowel	½" cementboard	Sealer
Masonry mixing tools	Metal snips	Lumber (2 × 4, 2 × 6)	Sandpaper
Mason's string	Wood float	Deck screws (2½, 3")	Level
Circular saw with masonry blade	Steel trowel	Silicone caulk	Doors
Work gloves	Drill with masonry bit	Stucco lath	Hinges
Eye and ear protection	Mortar mix	Release agent	Masonry anchors
Jigsaw with carbide grit blade	Reinforcing wire	Concrete mix	Grill
8 × 8 × 16" concrete block	Hammer	Base coat stucco	Gas fittings
Utility knife	Metal reinforcement		

This practical outdoor kitchen has just what the serious griller needs—a built-in grill and plenty of countertop space for preparing and serving meals. At just over 8 ft. long and about 3 ft. wide, the kitchen can fit almost anywhere on a standard concrete patio.

Construction Details

The basic structure of this kitchen consists of five courses of standard 8 × 8 × 16" concrete block. Two mortared layers of ½" cementboard serve as a base for the countertop. The 2"-thick poured concrete layer of the countertop extends 1½" beyond the rough block walls and covers the cementboard edges. The walls receive a two-coat stucco finish that can be tinted during the mixing or painted after it cures. Doors in the front of the cabinet provide access to storage space inside and to any utility connections for the grill. The kitchen's dimensions can easily be adjusted to accommodate a specific location, cooking equipment, or doors and additional amenities.

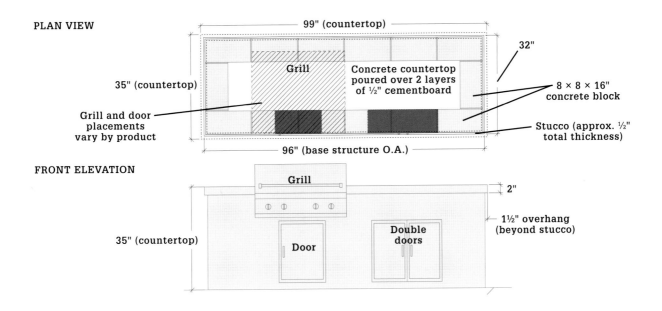

PLAN VIEW

99" (countertop)

Grill

Concrete countertop poured over 2 layers of ½" cementboard

32"

35" (countertop)

8 × 8 × 16" concrete block

Grill and door placements vary by product

Stucco (approx. ½" total thickness)

96" (base structure O.A.)

FRONT ELEVATION

Grill

2"

1½" overhang (beyond stucco)

35" (countertop)

Door

Double doors

Planning an Outdoor Kitchen Project ›

Whether you model your project after the one shown here or create your own design, there are a few critical factors to address as part of your initial planning:

Foundation: Check with your local building department about foundation requirements for your kitchen. Depending on the kitchen's size and location, you may be allowed to build on top of a standard four-inch-thick reinforced concrete patio slab, or you might need frost footings or a reinforced "floating footing."

Grill and door units: You'll need the exact dimensions of the grill, doors, and any other built-in features before you draw up your plans and start building. When shopping for equipment, keep in mind its utility requirements and the type of support system needed for the grill and other large units. Some grills are drop-in and are supported only by the countertop; others must be supported below with a noncombustible, load-bearing material such as concrete block or a poured concrete platform.

A grill gas line typically extends up into the cabinet space under the grill and is fitted with a shutoff valve.

Utility hookups: Grills fueled by natural gas require a plumbed gas line, and those with electric starters need an outdoor electrical circuit, both running into the kitchen cabinet. To include a kitchen sink, you'll need a dedicated water line and a drain connection (to the house system, directly to the city sewer, or possibly to a dry well on your property). Outdoor utilities are strictly governed by building codes, so check with the building department for requirements. Generally, the rough-in work for utilities is best left to professionals.

How to Build an Outdoor Kitchen

Pour the foundation or prepare the slab for the wall construction. To prepare an existing slab, clean the surface thoroughly to remove all dirt, oils, concrete sealers, and paint that could prevent a good bond with mortar.

Dry-lay the first course of block on the foundation to test the layout. If desired, use 2- or 4"-thick solid blocks under the door openings. Snap chalk lines to guide the block installation, and mark the exact locations of the door openings.

Set the first course of block into mortar. Cut blocks as needed for the door openings. Lay the second course, offsetting the joints with the first course in a running-bond pattern.

Continue laying up the wall, adding reinforcing wire or rebar if required by local building code. Instead of tooling the mortar joints for a concave profile, use a trowel to slice excess mortar from the blocks. This creates a flat surface that's easier to cover with stucco.

Install steel angle lintels to span over the door openings. If an opening is in line with a course of block, mortar the lintels in place on top of the block. Otherwise, use a circular saw with a masonry blade to cut channels for the horizontal leg of the angle. Lintels should span 6" beyond each side of an opening. Slip the lintel into the channels, and then fill the block cells containing the lintel with mortar to secure the lintel in place. Lay a bed of mortar on top of the lintels, and then set block into the mortar. Complete the final course of block in the cabinet and let the mortar cure.

Cut sheets of cementboard to match the outer dimensions of the block cabinet. Apply mortar to the tops of the cabinet blocks and then set one layer of cementboard into the mortar. If you will be installing a built-in grill or other accessories, make cutouts in the cementboard with a jigsaw with a carbide grit blade.

Cut pieces to fit for a second layer of cementboard. Apply a bed of mortar to the top of the first panel and then lay the second layer pieces on top, pressing them into the mortar so the surfaces are level. Let the mortar cure.

(continued)

To create a 1½" overhang for the countertop, build a perimeter band of 2 × 4 lumber; this will serve as the base of the concrete form. Cut the pieces to fit tightly around the cabinet along the top. Fasten the pieces together at their ends with 3" screws so their top edges are flush with the cementboard.

Cut vertical 2 × 4 supports to fit snugly between the foundation and the bottom of the 2 × 4 band. Install a support at the ends of each wall and evenly spaced in between. Secure each support with angled screws driven into the band boards.

Build the sides of the countertop form with 2 × 6s cut to fit around the 2 × 4 band. Position the 2 × 6s so their top edges are 2" above the cementboard and fasten them to the band with 2½" screws.

Form the opening for the grill using 2 × 6 side pieces (no overhang inside opening). Support the edges of the cementboard along the grill cutout with cleats attached to the 2 × 6s. Add vertical supports as needed under the cutout to keep the form from shifting under the weight of the concrete.

12

Cut a sheet of stucco lath to fit into the countertop form, leaving a 2" space along the inside perimeter of the form. Remove the lath and set it aside. Seal the form joints with a fine bead of silicone caulk and smooth with a finger. After the caulk dries, coat the form boards (not the cementboard) with vegetable oil or other release agent.

13

Dampen the cementboard with a mist of water. Mix a batch of countertop mix, adding color if desired. Working quickly, fill along the edges of the form with concrete, carefully packing it down into the overhang portion by hand.

14

Fill the rest of the form halfway up with an even layer of concrete. Lay the stucco lath on top, and then press it lightly into the concrete with a float. Add the remaining concrete so it's flush with the tops of the 2 × 6s.

15

Tap along the outsides of the form with a hammer to remove air bubbles trapped against the inside edges. Screed the top of the concrete with a straight 2 × 4 riding along the form sides. Add concrete as needed to fill in low spots so the surface is perfectly flat.

(continued)

16

After the bleed water disappears, float the concrete with a wood or magnesium float. The floated surface should be flat and smooth but will still have a somewhat rough texture. Be careful not to overfloat and draw water to the surface.

17

A few hours after floating, finish the countertop as desired. A few passes with a steel finishing trowel yields the smoothest surface. Hold the leading edge of the trowel up and work in circular strokes. Let the concrete set for a while between passes.

18

Moist-cure the countertop with a fine water mist for three to five days. Remove the form boards. If desired, smooth the countertop edges with an abrasive brick and/or a diamond pad or sandpaper. After the concrete cures, apply a food-safe sealer to help prevent staining.

19

Prepare for door installation in the cabinet. Outdoor cabinet doors are usually made of stainless steel and typically are installed by hanging hinges or flanges with masonry anchors. Drill holes for masonry anchors in the concrete block, following the door manufacturer's instructions.

Surface Voids ▶

Honeycombs or air voids can be filled using a cement slurry of cement and water applied with a rubber float. If liquid cement color was used in your countertop concrete mix, color should be added to the wet cement paste. Some experimentation will be necessary.

20

Finish installing and hanging the doors. Test the door operations and make sure to caulk around the edges with high-quality silicone caulk. *Note: Doors shown here are best installed before the stucco finish is applied to the cabinet. Other doors may be easier to install following a different sequence.*

21

To finish the cabinet walls, begin by dampening the contrete block and then applying a ⅜"-thick base coat of stucco. Apply an even layer over the walls; then smooth the surface with a wood float and moist-cure the stucco for 48 hours or as directed by the manufacturer.

22

Apply a finish coat of tinted stucco that's at least ⅛" thick. Evenly saturate the base coat stucco surface with water prior to applying the finish coat. Texture the surface as desired. Moist-cure the stucco for several days as directed.

23

Set the grill into place, make the gas connection, and then check it carefully for leaks. Permanently install the grill following the manufacturer's directions. The joints around grills are highly susceptible to water intrusion; seal them thoroughly with an approved caulk to help keep moisture out of the cabinet space below.

Outdoor Kitchen Walls & Countertop

Loaded with convenient work surfaces and a dedicated grill space, the outdoor kitchen has changed backyard grilling forever. This roomy kitchen can be the perfect addition to any patio or garden retreat. It's made entirely of concrete pavers and not only looks great, it's also incredibly easy to build.

The design of this kitchen comes from a manufacturer that supplies all of the necessary masonry materials on two pallets. As shown, the project's footprint is about 98 × 109 inches and includes a 58-inch-wide space for setting in a grill. Square columns can provide work surfaces on either side of the grill, so you'll want to keep them conveniently close, but if you need a little more or a little less room for your grill, you can simply adjust the number of blocks that go into the front wall section enclosing the grill alcove.

Opposite the grill station is a 32-inch-tall countertop capped with large square pavers, or patio stones, for a finished look. This countertop has a lower surface for food prep and a higher surface for serving or dining. A low side wall connects the countertop with the grill area and adds just the right amount of enclosure to complete the kitchen space.

Tools & Materials ›

Masonry outdoor kitchen kit (concrete wall block, concrete patio stones)	Level
	Caulk gun
	Exterior-grade concrete adhesive
Chalk line	Tape measure
Framing square	Eye and ear protection
Straight board	Work gloves

This all-masonry outdoor kitchen comes ready to assemble on any solid patio surface, or you can build it over a prepared gravel base anywhere in your landscape (check with the manufacturer for base requirements). For a custom design, similar materials are available to purchase separately and the installation would be more or less the same as shown here. Discuss the project with the manufacturer for specifics. If you decide to build just a part of this kitchen (the bar, for example), review the setup and site prep steps at the beginning of this project.

How to Build the Outdoor Kitchen

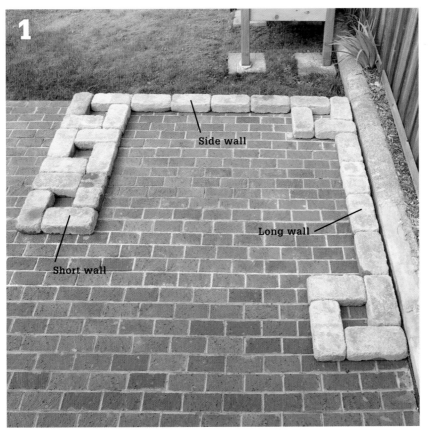

Dry-lay the project on the installation surface. This overview of the first course of blocks shows how the kitchen is constructed with five columns and two wall sections. Laying out the first course carefully and making sure the wall sections are square ensures the rest of the project will go smoothly.

Create squared reference lines for the kitchen walls after you remove the dry-laid blocks. Snap a chalk line representing the outside face of the front wall. Mark the point where the side wall will meet the front wall. Place a framing square at the mark and trace a perpendicular line along the leg of the square. Snap a chalk line along the pencil line to represent the side wall, or use the edge of a patio as this boundary (as shown). To confirm that the lines are square, mark the frontwall line 36" from the corner and the sidewall line 48" from the corner. The distance between the marks should be 60". If not, re-snap one of the chalk lines until the measurements work out.

(continued)

Begin laying the first course of block. Starting in the 90° corner of the chalk lines, set four blocks at right angles to begin the corner column. Make sure all blocks are placed together tightly. Set the long wall with blocks laid end to end, followed by another column.

Finish laying the first course, including two more columns, starting at the side wall. Use a straight board as a guide to make sure the columns form a straight line. To check for square, measure between the long wall and the short wall at both ends; the measurements should be equal. Adjust the short-wall columns as needed.

Set the second course. Add the second course of blocks to each of the columns, rotating the pattern 90° to the first course. Set the blocks for the long and side walls, leaving about a 2" gap in between the corner column and the first block. Set the remaining wall blocks with the same gap so the blocks overlap the joints in the first course.

Set the third course. Lay the third-course blocks using the same pattern as in the first course. For appearance and stability, make sure the faces of the blocks are flush with one another and that the walls and columns are plumb. Use a level to align the blocks and check for plumb.

Install the remaining courses. The higher courses of wall block are glued in place. Set the courses in alternating patterns, as before, gluing each block in place with concrete adhesive.

Build the short wall overhang. Starting at one end of the short wall, glue wall blocks along the tops of the columns with concrete adhesive. Position blocks perpendicular to the length of the short wall, overhanging the columns by 3".

Complete the short wall top. Create the counter surface for the short wall by gluing patio stones to the tops of the columns and overhanging blocks. Position the stones for the lower surface against the ends of the overhanging blocks. Position the upper-surface stones so they extend beyond the overhanging blocks slightly on the outside ends and a little more so on the overhanging blocks.

Cap the corner columns. Finish the two corner columns with wall blocks running parallel to the side wall. Glue the cap pieces in place on the columns using concrete adhesive. Make sure the blocks are fitted tightly together.

Firepit

A firepit is a backyard focal point and gathering spot. The one featured here is constructed around a metal liner, which will keep the fire pit walls from overheating and cracking if cooled suddenly by rain or a bucket of water. The liner here is a section of 36-inch-diameter corrugated culvert pipe. Check local codes for stipulations on pit area size. Many codes require a 20-foot-diameter pit area.

Ashlar wall stones add character to the fire pit walls, but you can use any type of stone, including cast concrete retaining wall blocks. You'll want to prep the base for the seating area as you dig the firepit to be sure both rest on the same level plane.

Tools & Materials ▸

Wheelbarrow
Landscape paint
String and stakes
Spade
Metal pipe
Landscape edging
Level
Garden rake

Plate vibrator
Metal firepit liner
Compactable gravel
Top-dressing rock
   (trap rock)
Wall stones
Eye and ear protection
Work gloves

Some pointers to consider when using your firepit include: 1) Make sure there are no bans or restrictions in effect; 2) Evaluate wind conditions and avoid building a fire if winds are heavy and/or blowing toward your home; 3) Keep shovels, sand, water, and a fire extinguisher nearby; 4) Extinguish fire with water and never leave the firepit unattended.

Cross Section: Firepit

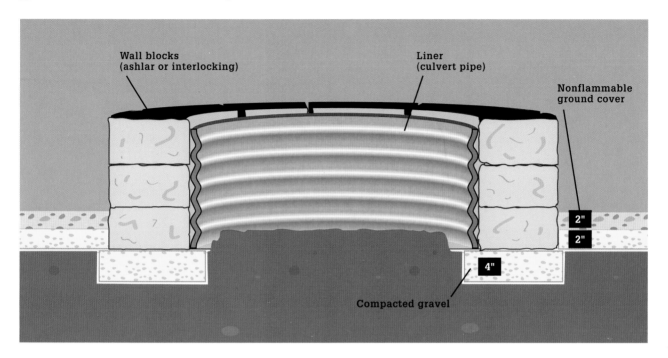

Wall blocks
(ashlar or interlocking)

Liner
(culvert pipe)

Nonflammable
ground cover

2"

2"

4"

Compacted gravel

Plan View: Firepit

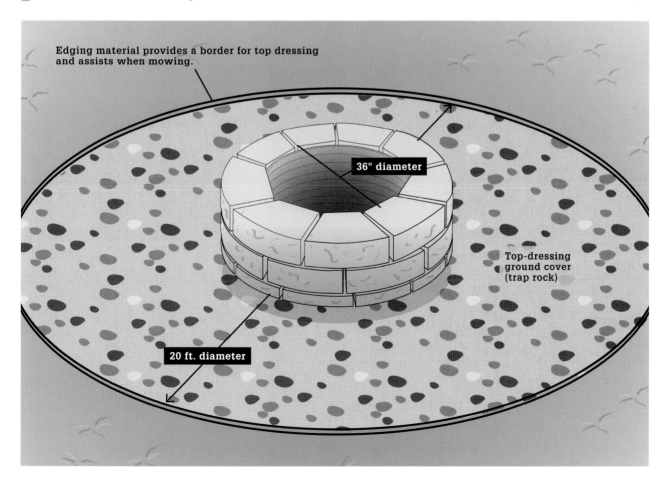

Edging material provides a border for top dressing
and assists when mowing.

36" diameter

Top-dressing
ground cover
(trap rock)

20 ft. diameter

How to Build a Firepit

10 ft. radius

Outline the location for your firepit and the firepit safety area by drawing concentric circles with landscape paint using a string and stake for guidance.

Remove a 4"-deep layer of sod and dirt in the firepit and safety areas (the depth of the excavation depends on what materials you're installing in the safety zone.)

Dig a 4"-deep trench for the perimeter stones that will ring the pit liner.

Fill the trench for the perimeter stones with compactable gravel and tamp thoroughly. Then scatter gravel to within 2½" of the paver edging top throughout the project area. It is not necessary to tamp this layer at this time.

Place your metal fire ring so it is level on the gravel layer and centered around the center pipe.

6

Arrange the first course of wall blocks around the fire ring. Keep gaps even and check with a level, adding or removing gravel as needed.

7

Install the second course of retaining wall block, taking care to evenly stagger the vertical joints on the first and second courses. Add the remaining courses.

8

Compact the gravel in the seating/safety area using a rental plate vibrator.

9

Place and compact a layer of top-dressing rock in the seating/safety area to complete the firepit.

Backyard Theater

The classic drive-in theater isn't the thriving weekend hotspot that it was not so long ago, but you can recapture the pleasure of watching a movie outside on a summer night by building your own outdoor home theater—and it doesn't have to cost a fortune.

Thanks to advancing technology in home electronics, there is a wide variety of equipment for sale that is capable of large-screen image display. Which equipment you choose should depend on how many people will be watching, how much space you have, and of course how much money you want to spend. Plug-and-play systems with an inflatable screen, a projector, a DVD player, and speakers are available for under $2,000, but you can reduce that price considerably if you already have a home theater from which you can borrow components or if your yard is already wired for sound. If you are a true DIYer, you can purchase a digital projector for as little as $100 and build a theater around it for practically nothing. Note, though, that a digital projector is an image output device only; you'll need to hook it up to an input device such as a DVD or Blu-ray player.

Your backyard movie screen can be as large as your projector can handle: 4 × 7 ft., 4½ × 8 ft., 7 × 12 ft. and 9 × 16 ft. are some common sizes. The screen itself can be anything from reflective photographer's fabric to a smooth wall on the side of the house (naturally, the material will impact picture quality). Make sure you have sufficient space for your projector before you set the screen up by checking the recommended throw distance (distance of the projector from the screen) and recommended seating area. You can check these figures online at sites that sell projectors.

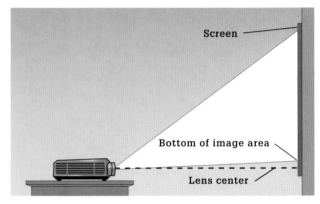

Projectors beam out an offset image so the image won't be obstructed by the table the projector is sitting on or the ceiling it is mounted to. The degree of offset can usually be manipulated within a limited range to conform to your preferences for screen height and mounting height. However, using the maximum offset can cause some image distortion.

Create a better alternative to another night in front of the TV by setting up an outdoor movie theater in your backyard.

Terms You Should Know ▸

Aspect ratio: The aspect ratio refers to the proportions of the projected image. Standard televisions project a 4:3 aspect ratio image (4 units wide to 3 units high). Many newer models (high-definition TV in particular) use the narrower 16:9 ratio (16 units wide to 9 units high), which is based on a typical motion picture screen shape. Most home projection theaters have a native 16:9 ratio because they tend to feature movies that were originally shot in this mode. But if you intend to use your theater for viewing TV or recordings of shows shot for TV, you should look into the 4:3 aspect ratio.

Resolution: The resolution of a projector refers to the maximum number of image pixels it can produce: the more pixels, the crisper the image. Among digital projectors, you have three typical resolution options available. The numbers noted refer to the number of available pixels in a horizontal line by the number in a vertical line.

854 by 480 ("480p"): These are relatively low-resolution projectors, but the 480 pixels in the vertical line matches the output of regular TV or DVD, so if you don't plan to get into the high-definition game, this entry-level projector may work for you.

1280 by 720 ("720p"): The most common resolution for 16:9 home projectors, they can handle high-definition digital signals and many are quite affordable.

1920 by 1080 ("1080p"): The sharpest picture quality available, these ultra-high definition projectors are designed to handle HD DVD and Blu-ray discs without any image degradation. These are the most expensive projectors.

Brightness, contrast, and throw are other variables you should acquaint yourself with if you're looking into a higher end projector.

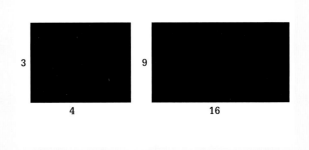

Front-Projection TVs

When you think of projection televisions, you probably have in mind three large colored lenses in a box the size of a small refrigerator. Known as CRT projectors, these models generally require professional installation and are quite expensive. But the digital revolution has impacted the world of front-projection TVs. Today, the projector market is being taken over by digital projectors in a variety of formats. The most common is LCD (liquid crystal display), a technology that is also being used extensively in rear-projection televisions. A slightly more expensive digital format is DLP (digital light processing), a proprietary technology owned by Texas Instruments. With the new technology, projectors have been trimmed down to as small as five pounds, making them portable and more flexible for home use.

Today's smaller, more affordable front-projection systems offer crisp digital images and are easily installed.

Make an Outdoor Picture Screen

Inventive DIYers have been known to put together reasonably good outdoor theaters with used projectors, old stereo speakers, and a white dropcloth or sheet tacked to the side of the house. Without going to quite such extremes of thriftiness, you can still save money by making your own screen using black-out cloth or theater screen material (available from fabric stores) or by painting hardboard or other smooth sheetgoods.

Unless special weatherproof materials are used, screens should be stored indoors when not in use to keep them in good condition, though an occasional day outside won't hurt. This means that whatever the size, the screen should be light enough that it can be moved without too much difficulty, and either small enough to fit indoors or made so it can be folded or rolled up. An example of a smallish, but easily portable, screen follows.

Screen option: Cut a piece of thin sheet stock, such as ¼" hardboard, to 84" long and then paint it using white acrylic primer and white screen paint (Behr SilverScreen paint, #770E-2 is one brand). Attach black fabric or tape around the perimeter and set up the screen in your yard.

How to Build a Portable Movie Screen

Make a frame with mitered corners for the screen, using 1 × 4 pine or cedar. The inside dimensions once the frame is built should equal the planned picture size. In the project seen here, the dimensions are 4 ft. high and 7 ft. wide. Fasten corners with finish nails or biscuits.

Buy some black felt and cut it into strips to apply to the frame. The felt improves picture quality (to the eye) and does not reflect light. Cut it into strips slightly longer than each board, and wide enough to wrap around the back.

Affix the felt strips to the frame with spray adhesive, tucking the backs of the strips behind the frame. Staple the strips to the back for extra strength. Stretch the felt tight as you set it into the adhesive, then trim the ends with a razor knife, following the miter.

Cut a piece of blackout cloth from a 54"-wide roll and lay it out flat on the backside of the frame, centered over the frame opening. Stretch the cloth tight and tack it to the frame with staples. Then, nail retainer strips over the edges, trapping the edge between the retainers and the back of the frame.

Wildlife Observation

One of the pleasures of having a backyard is watching wildlife wander through. Although birds and butterflies are considered the most desirable visitors, some four-legged species, such as deer or rabbits, might be welcome guests in your yard as well.

By far the best way to attract wildlife is to provide feeders. Put out a bird feeder in a barren backyard and within days (if not sooner), birds of all types from miles around will be flying in for a meal. Seeds and nuts spread on the ground will attract squirrels and chipmunks, but also larger foraging animals if there

are any in the area. A flower garden quickly becomes a magnet for local bees, butterflies, moths, dragonflies, ladybugs and dozens of other species. And the more you watch them, the more they reveal.

Because so much wildlife is skittish and will disappear at the first hint of human motion, some homeowners have taken a page from the hunting handbook and built observation blinds. These camouflage screens are installed near patio doors and windows to hide observers while still offering sightlines through strategically cut holes in the screening.

This bamboo blind structure provides critical cover for watchers of wildlife.

Bamboo Observation Blind

Wild animals and birds are easily spooked, and no matter how attractive the food is, they will stay hidden if they see people moving around in the vicinity. If you don't have a convenient picture window to watch from you can construct an observation blind that will help

you get closer. The blind is constructed from rolled bamboo fencing attached to a 2 × 4 frame, with a small area cut out for viewing. If possible, place the blind near trees or bushes, and add climbing vines and other plantings after it's installed to make it blend in better.

Tools & Materials ▸

(per section)
¾ × 6" × 6' rolled
   bamboo fencing
   cut to 34¼" wide

(2) 4 × 4" × 8' PT posts
(5) 2 × 4" × 8' PT lumber
(8) 2 × 4" fence brackets
2½" deck screws

1½" galv. casing nails
Joist hanger nails
Pea gravel (two 60# bags)
Jigsaw

Circular saw
Drill
Eye and ear protection
Work gloves

How to Build a Bamboo Blind

Build the framework. Install a 4 × 4 post at each end of the blind, a minimum of 2 ft. deep. Leave 73" of the post projecting above ground. Fill the post holes with gravel or concrete. Nail the fence brackets in place, and then set the 2 × 4s into the brackets. Add a center stile to stabilize the rails.

Attach the bamboo fabric. First, cut the bamboo fencing into two 34¼" sections and cut out the viewing areas (3 × 8") with a jigsaw after testing the viewing height while sitting on a chair. Predrill the bamboo and nail it in place, nailing it every 6". Add additional sides as needed for concealment. Attach the bamboo fabric to the framework with galvanized casing nails.

Bird Nest Box Dimensions ▸

Different bird species prefer different-sized nesting boxes. Some species, like robins, will not nest in boxes, but prefer platforms on which to build their nests.

Keeping predators and invasive species, like sparrows, from invading nesting boxes is important. Drilling the proper size entrance hole protects your house from becoming a home to sparrows or squirrels. Do not use perches, as these allow predatory birds to sit and wait for adults and nestlings to emerge.

The following chart shows nesting box dimensions for common bird species.

Nest Box Dimensions

Species	Box floor	Box height	Hole height	Hole diameter	Box placement
Eastern Bluebird	5 × 5"	8 to 12"	6 to 10"	1½"	4 to 6 ft.
Chickadees	4 × 4"	8 to 10"	6 to 8"	1⅛"	4 to 15 ft.
Titmice	4 × 4"	10 to 12"	6 to 10"	1¼"	5 to 15 ft.
Red-breasted Nuthatch	4 × 4"	8 to 10"	6 to 8"	1¼"	5 to 15 ft.
White-breasted Nuthatch	4 × 4"	8 to 10"	6 to 8"	1⅜"	5 to 15 ft.
Northern Flicker	7 × 7"	16 to 18"	14 to 16"	2½"	6 to 20 ft.
Yellow-bellied Sapsucker	5 × 5"	12 to 15"	9 to 12"	1½"	10 to 20 ft.
House Wrens	4 × 4"	6 to 8"	4 to 6"	1¼"	5 to 10 ft.
Carolina Wren	4 × 4"	6 to 8"	4 to 6"	1½"	5 to 10 ft.
Wood Ducks	10 × 18"	10 to 24"	12 to 16"	4"	10 to 20 ft.

Birdfeeder with Motion-Activated Camera

Getting good photographs of the birds and animals that visit your backyard can add a whole new level of enjoyment to wildlife observation. Motion-activated cameras give you a record of everything that visits the feeders when you're not around—even at night, if you purchase a camera with infrared night vision.

If you don't have a tree near your feeder to attach the camera to, you can build a feeder stand with a camera holder set at just the right distance from the feeder, then capture still photos or short videos whenever a bird comes in for a meal.

Tools & Materials ▸

(4) 4 × 4 × 24"
(2) 4 × 4 × 17"
(1) 2 × 4 × 84"
(2) 1 × 4 × 72"
(2) 1 × 4 × 3"
(2) 2 × 4 × 3½"
(2) 4 × 4" L-brackets
(8) ⁵⁄₁₆ × 6" lag bolts plus washers
(1) ¼ × 1½" bolt
(2) nuts
Cord

(2) ⅜ × 10" carriage bolts, nuts, washers
(8) 1⅝" deck screws
(6) 2½" deck screws
Construction adhesive
Motion-activated camera (see Resources, page 237)
Drill/driver
Eye and ear protection
Work gloves

Get close-up, highly detailed photos of birds by attaching a motion-activated camera to your bird feeder.

How to Build a Birdfeeder with Camera

Assemble the base and the 2 × 4 × 84 pole, adding construction adhesive at the joints. Screw the 2 × 4 to the 4 × 4s, keeping the screws to the side, to hold it in place until all the 4 × 4s are drilled and bolted in place.

Attach the crossbars. Predrill, glue, and screw the 1 × 4 × 72 crossbars that support the feeders to the 2 × 4 pole, then add 2 × 4 × 3½ fillers at each end to strengthen the 1 × 4s and keep them from warping.

Hang the feeders. Drill a ¼" diameter hole in the 1 × 4 × 3 filler, then feed cord through the hole. Knot one end so it won't pull through. Hang the feeder on the other end, then move the feeder back and forth until you find the right distance for a good photo.

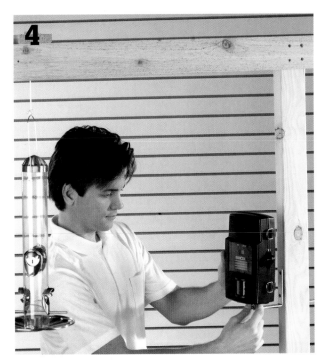

Mount the camera. Attach 4 × 4" metal angle brackets to each side of the pole, level with the feeder. Mount the camera on the bracket with a ¼" × 1½" bolt. *Note: The bolt diameter and thread size should match the female threaded hole for a tripod mount in your camera base.*

Backyard Pools & Spas

Swimming pools have long been an important part of backyard recreation, especially in warmer parts of the country. This overview of inground and above-ground swimming pools and spas explains the difference between concrete, vinyl, and fiberglass pools and shows the basics about how each type is constructed. There's also a discussion of more DIY-friendly, above-ground pools including heavy-duty reinforced vinyl models that can be set up or taken down in hours.

This chapter is intended as a guide for the hands-on property owner who is considering enhancing his or her yard with a swimming pool or hot tub. Inground pools and large above-ground pools require heavy equipment and are usually best installed by professionals, though cleaning and maintenance are not difficult for homeowners. However, ambitious DIYers can install smaller above-ground pools and spas without serious difficulty.

In this chapter:

- Choosing a Pool or Spa
- Concrete Pools & Spas
- Vinyl-lined Pools
- Fiberglass Shell Pools
- Above-ground Pools
- Spas & Hot Tubs
- Pool & Spa Safety

Choosing a Pool or Spa

If you're shopping for a pool or spa (or both) for your yard, the first step is to define why and how you'll use these lifestyle assets. Without a doubt, pools and spas offer a variety of benefits, often in combination. For instance, they can serve a personal need for relaxation while enhancing the resale value of your home. Defining and prioritizing the importance of a pool or spa as a component of your lifestyle will help refine your plans, aiding the decision to add or remodel one or both and helping you gain a better understanding and appreciation for taking care of that investment. Consider the following benefits of a pool or spa:

Entertainment. Most pools and spas for private home use are built and used for entertainment, whether alone, as a couple, as a family, or with friends, neighbors, and extended family.

Relaxation. Coupled with entertainment, there's the benefit of relaxation, of cooling off in the water on a hot summer day, or enjoying a soak in the evening.

Housing value. Homes with an in-ground pool add about 8 percent to the value of a residential property, according to a recent study by the National Association of Realtors; adding an in-ground pool to a $200,000 home, for instance, appreciates its value by $16,000 as soon as you fill it with water and fire up the pumps. (The same study found that above-ground pools add no discernible value to a home.)

Exercise. Swimming is one of the best low-impact aerobic exercises you can get.

Design element. Some pools are designed and built mostly as water features in the garden. Whether still or with movement facilitated by a pump and filter system, decorative pools bring the soothing and attractive element of water to the garden and become places to reflect alone or gather as a group.

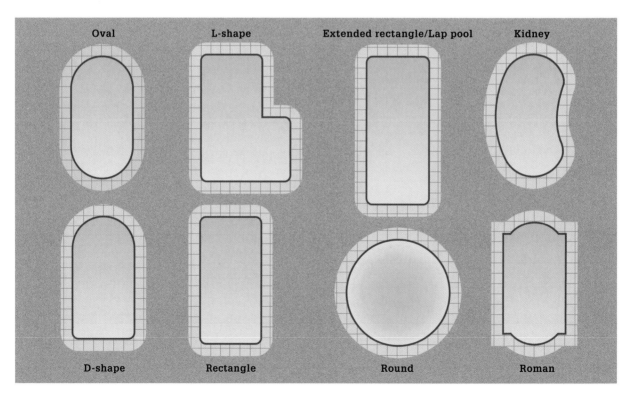

Typical swimming pool shapes give you several recognizable design options, but if you're using a vinyl liner or concrete pool walls and floor, the design possibilities are practically limitless.

A custom spa that's integrated with the pool offers the ultimate in luxury and convenience. And with the right combination of styles, shapes and colors, it can be visually stunning as well.

Concrete Pools & Spas

The traditional residential pool (if there is such a thing) is an in-ground pool with concrete walls and a concrete deck. While there are several advantages to going the concrete route, especially if you live in a temperate climate, more modern shell options have been taking over the home pool market in recent years.

The excavation for the concrete pool must be outfitted with reinforcement (typically metal rebar) to strengthen the concrete shell. When finished, the web of vertical and horizontal rebar resembles a metal cage in the same shape as the excavation, held about four inches out from the dirt sides and bottom of the pool. Other features, such as steps or integral seating, might be formed with plywood or rebar in preparation for concrete. In addition, a thicker "bond beam" along the top of the walls is formed with rebar to support the pool deck and coping.

Concurrently, the contractor will install (or "rough in") the pool or spa's recirculation system behind and within the rebar cage. This includes skimmer openings, the main drain, suction valves, and any automated cleaning, water feature, and/or lighting conduits that are to be run underground from the pool or spa structure to the equipment set nearby. Once properly installed, the pipes, wires, and other conduits are located or "stubbed up" near the location of the equipment set, to be connected later; their openings in the pool shell are covered or otherwise protected during the construction process to keep dirt,

A poured concrete pool with concrete coping can take on just about any shape you please. Although concrete is more common in nonresidential pools and in areas with a warmer climate, the only good reason not to consider one is that they cost at least 50% more to install than a vinyl-lined pool of the same size.

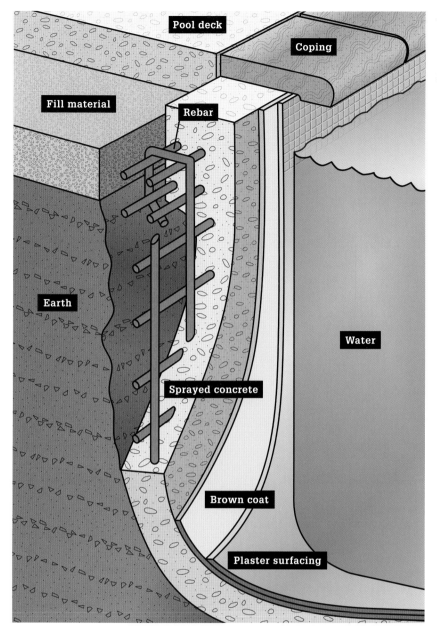

Pool deck

Coping

Fill material

Rebar

Earth

Sprayed concrete

Water

Brown coat

Plaster surfacing

A concrete pool is built much like a building foundation, with reinforced concrete walls and floor. Most concrete pools are coated with a surface layer of gunite or shotcrete.

construction debris, trash, pests, and concrete from clogging the system.

In recent years, pool builders have relied on one of two spray-applied methods (gunite and shotcrete) to create the shell of a concrete pool, all but replacing standard poured concrete and concrete masonry units in pool and spa construction. These two spray-applied methods are more time-efficient and appropriate for concrete pool and spa building. They are easier to control, faster to apply, adhere better to the excavated and reinforced sidewalls without significant sloughing (compared to traditional poured concrete methods), and enable the greatest amount of design flexibility.

After the pool walls are created, a cement-based finish is applied to the raw concrete surface. Ceramic tile is often added along the top several inches of the sidewalls as a decorative feature and as an easy-to-clean material at the waterline in plaster-finished pools and spas.

Once the finish is cured (requiring perhaps another week), the pool or spa builder or equipment installer finishes the systems rough-in with skimmer flaps, drain covers, outlet fittings, and, of course, the equipment set nearby. When the deck and any other landscape or integral water features and finishes are completed, the pool or spa can be filled with water, cleaned and balanced, and enjoyed.

Vinyl-lined Pools

In-ground pools built using a vinyl liner are less expensive and faster to install than a concrete pool. Often called "packaged" pools, they are available in a limited—if increasing—variety of shapes and sizes, and are typically delivered with all the necessary components to complete the project.

Instead of reinforced concrete, an interlocking system of support members creates the structure of a vinyl-lined pool. These components, usually L-shaped, are engineered and made of aluminum, steel, plastic, or stainless steel; a contractor may also use concrete blocks or treated wood for below-grade projects. Regardless, these structural components create a solid shell for a thick, watertight vinyl membrane.

For in-ground, vinyl-lined pools and spas, the excavation phase of the project is similar to that of a concrete pool, except that the hole must be dug large enough to accommodate the buttresses of the sidewall components, as well as the rough-in of the recirculation system and any accessory features serving the pool.

The pool bottom is leveled and covered (and leveled again) with sand, cement, or vermiculite to reduce the chance of tearing the liner. With the structure secure and level, the system's rough-ins in place, and the pool or spa bottom ready, the liner is carefully unfolded and/or unrolled and gently pulled to the sides. The process is arduous, requiring several people and, especially toward the end, a good deal of strength. Folds, if any, are spread out or cut away.

With the liner securely in place and molded to any steps, seating, or other integral features (typically accommodated in the factory to maintain the liner's structural integrity), a contractor installs and connects the plumbing and lighting finishes and the equipment set, making the pool or spa ready for water. Then the contractor fills in the excavated area behind the structural members with dirt (called backfill) to balance the pressure on both sides of the pool or spa. The backfill also forms the base for the deck and coping material surrounding the pool or spa.

The main concern about vinyl liners is their vulnerability to chemicals and UV rays, especially if the water chemistry is routinely unbalanced and unsanitary. Dry chlorine, for instance, must be completely dissolved in the pool water, perhaps mixed in a separate, non-metal bucket of water before being placed in the pool.

As with any pool or spa, a regular schedule of careful and appropriate maintenance goes a long way to preserving the integrity and value of your investment. Care for it correctly, and a vinyl liner can last up to 15 years before it needs to be replaced from normal wear and tear.

Vinyl pool liners are taking over much of the residential pool market because they are the least expensive system and they offer low maintenance. Because the pressure from the weight of the water maintains the pool shape, in-ground vinyl pools cannot be drained.

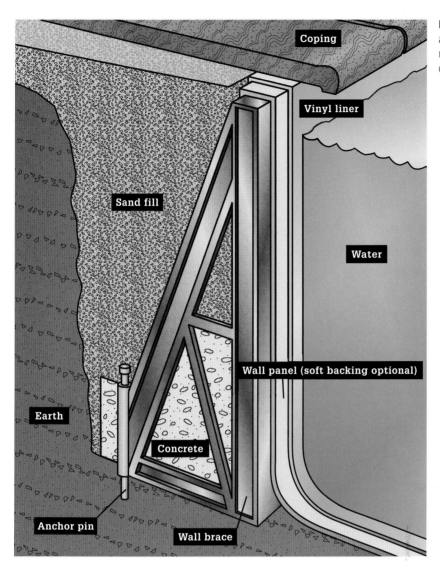

Coping

Vinyl liner

Sand fill

Water

Wall panel (soft backing optional)

Earth

Concrete

Anchor pin

Wall brace

In-ground pools with a vinyl liner
are low in maintenance, but the liners usually require replacement after 15 years or so.

Vinyl liners are made in a dizzying array of colors and patterns that you may choose from when ordering your new pool or a replacement liner.

Installation of a Vinyl-lined Pool ▸

A swimming pool with a vinyl liner is a relatively fast pool type for professionals to install. The hole that is excavated for the pool has very low tolerance, however, so great pains are taken to get the shape leveled and finished. Any imperfections in the excavation will show through on the finished product.

Once the pool installation is complete, the pool deck is added. Often, the deck is made of poured concrete with integral coping that covers the tops of the pool support walls. Other materials, such as flagstone or concrete pavers, also may be used for the deck surface.

The site is excavated to the sidewall depth, then the walls are positioned and braced.

The excavation is completed to final depth at the deep end, usually with a backhoe.

Plumbing and equipment are hooked up and the shape of the excavation is refined. A concrete footing is poured around the perimeter of the pool wall.

Soft wall panels are installed on the excavation walls to provide cushion so the vinyl is less likely to tear. An additional cushion layer may be installed between the wall and the vinyl liner.

The vinyl liner is placed into the pool excavation and attached to the tops of the support walls. The area behind the walls is backfilled once all of the pool connections are made.

Fiberglass Shell Pools

Fiberglass is a significantly less popular pool type than concrete or vinyl, but the great majority of spas and hot tubs have a fiberglass shell. In-ground fiberglass pools are very limited in their available sizes and shapes. This is mostly because, as factory-made shells, they must be built within certain dimensions to be safely transportable.

The excavation process for a fiberglass pool is similar to concrete and vinyl-lined projects; as with the latter, the contractor digs a hole a bit larger than the shell to accommodate the system rough-in components and to allow the installation crew to properly level the bottom and backfill against the outside of the pool walls.

Once the excavated area has been prepared and its bottom leveled or shaped to match that of the pool shell as closely as possible, the pool is hoisted from the delivery truck with a crane and carefully placed in the hole. Rarely will the first placement be perfect; more likely, the crew (using the crane) will have to lift the pool out and refine the excavation to ensure that the bottom of the pool is completely and reliably supported.

Eventually, the pool shell is unstrapped, steadied by temporary bracing, and connected to the recirculation system rough-in and above-ground equipment. The pool is filled with water and backfilled at the same time to balance the pressure on both sides of the walls. The backfill is typically wet sand that fills voids between the exterior shell walls and the excavated hole. To provide stability and drainage for the coping and deck material, some contractors lay a bed of crushed rock for the top four inches or so of the backfill.

In-ground fiberglass pools typically are more expensive than comparably sized and standard-shaped concrete pools. However, above-ground fiberglass pools are more cost-competitive, primarily because there is no excavation required and, in the case of spas, the pump, filter, heater, and other system components are usually contained in the package from the factory. They are also smaller than other in-ground pools, requiring less water and fewer chemicals (and less expense) to maintain.

As with any pool or spa, fiberglass is not immune to wear and tear. The inside gel-coat surface can become brittle and cracked from neglect and will wear out over time. Severe surface damage may even affect the fiberglass material behind the coating, requiring a patch that may necessitate re-excavation if it is serious enough to cause a leak. Fiberglass also cannot withstand a lot of weight on its edges; a pool deck or coping material, or stone edging that relies on the shell for structural support may buckle the fiberglass. As an alternative, fiberglass pool manufacturers are broadening the design options for the integral coping that's premolded into their products.

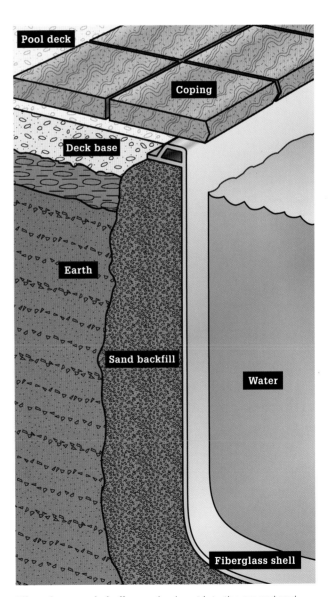

Fiberglass pool shells are simply set into the ground and wet sand is dumped in from above to backfill around the shell.

Above-ground Pools

Long perceived as the cheap alternative to in-ground pools, the pools that stake their claim above ground have improved dramatically in appearance, durability, and performance in recent years.

Resins are now the rule for exterior shell materials, providing one-piece finishes that not only open up design options in color and pattern, but last longer than their predecessors. Inside shells (usually flexible liners), meanwhile, feature factory-applied patterns that replicate the tiled waterline borders of concrete pools, among other finishes. Manufacturers are also creating perimeter top edges that are 10 inches wide, providing enough surface area (and the perception of bulk) to meet demand from consumers who don't want or cannot accommodate a full deck around the pool or spa.

Responding to smaller backyard lots in today's new housing landscape, above-ground pool makers have re-engineered the structural system to eliminate buttresses (the supports projecting from the exterior walls, as backfilling does for an in-ground pool), saving six feet or so in the overall width and length of the pool. Similarly, the latest above-ground pools are 50 inches or more deep to more closely resemble in-ground pool depths. Automation and better equipment have also crept into the market, and automatic cleaners and chlorinators are more common, along with more powerful pumps and filters.

To install an above-ground pool, you start by outlining and then leveling out the pool area to at least four feet beyond the pool footprint. Level the area by

Above-ground pools may lack some of the cachet of an in-ground pool, but they are much more affordable and much more practical for many homeowners.

Inflatable & Temporary Pools ▸

The last distinct category of pool construction is inflatable and temporary pools. These above-ground products are truly mobile, though often as big (if not as deep) as any other type of pool, and requiring just a flat, clean surface and a garden hose. More sophisticated models feature attachable pumps and filters to circulate and help clean the water, as well as covers, cleaning accessories, and repair kits that make it easier to maintain them during heavy seasonal and multi-year use.

As their name implies, inflatable pools feature sidewalls filled with air to create a vessel for water. Some sport inflatable top collars that pull the sidewalls up to their full height as the pool fills with water. Similarly, temporary pools feature flexible sidewalls held up and in place by strategically spaced structural members and

filled with water, and offer a consistent depth, usually about four feet.

Made with tough, thick vinyl (the thickest layer forming the bottom), inflatable and temporary pools can be up and ready to enjoy fast, and they tear down just as quickly. If they are to remain standing or filled for multiple uses or certainly a season, they can (and should) be sanitized and chemically balanced as a permanent pool or spa to maintain their integrity and value.

Primarily, however, inflatable and soft-sided pools are an inexpensive and easy way to enjoy the water, and can be stored and moved simply, making them ideal for renters and budget-conscious homeowners. Such pools are also not considered "real" or taxable property, as a more permanent pool or spa would be assessed, thus saving you a bit on your property taxes and homeowner insurance premiums.

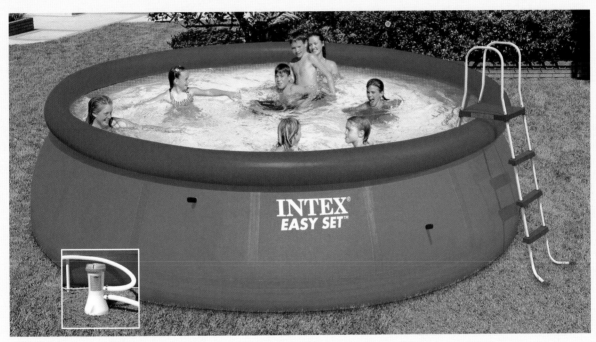

Inflatable and temporary pools are being made in ever-larger sizes, dramatically increasing their appeal for backyard use. A recirculating pump with a small filter (inset) is the only equipment that accompanies most inflatable pools.

removing high ground, taking care not to disturb the ground that remains behind. Then, you assemble a framework made from base rail plates that support uprights. A layer of sand is laid on the entire area, to create a smooth bottom and protect the pool bottom from rocks and sharp objects in the ground.

Once the framework, including the upright panels, is in place and the sand bed is laid, the liner

fabric is draped over the frame, then held in place with plastic edging. Then, the top plates, rails and cover are installed according to the pool instructions. The pumps and skimmer are attached as the pool is being filled. Typically, you'll need to make cutouts in the liner for the hookups. Make cutouts in the liner and install the skimmer and pump when the pool is a third full.

Spas & Hot Tubs

All of the three main pool construction methods (concrete, vinyl, fiberglass) can be used to create a backyard spa. Hot tubs, a closely related fixture, are deep, wood-slat built vessels that are installed above ground and have a barrel appearance that was popularized in the 1970s.

SPAS

Like pools, spas can be built into the ground or set above ground. Increasingly, in-ground spas are integrated in their design and construction with an adjacent pool, allowing users to soak and cool down, perhaps several times, without necessarily getting out of the water. Typically, such combinations are built using the concrete method described for pools. In such cases, the pool and spa also tend to share the equipment set and recirculation and filtering process, though pool experts often advise separate systems to accommodate the different chemical and sanitation needs of pools and spas. Like the pool itself, a concrete spa can be designed, built, and finished to just about any shape, size, depth, and appearance, and it can integrate features including spill-overs into the pool or waterfalls of recirculated water cascading into the spa from a rock formation.

An in-ground vinyl-lined or fiberglass pool and spa combination, meanwhile, is rare, given that both the pool and the spa require separate excavations (and thus would not be truly integrated, as a concrete combination can). More likely, a portable, self-contained spa is installed to complement an in-ground vinyl-lined or fiberglass pool, perhaps excavated, to bring its deck flush to that of the adjacent pool's.

That said, a fiberglass spa shell, designed, manufactured, and roughed-in for the multiple hydrojets and integral seating of a portable spa, can be set in-ground like a pool, and finished and landscaped on grade to replicate a concrete project.

Jetted home spas may be set into the ground or into a deck, but often they are trimmed with decorative wood skirting to conceal the plumbing and the unappealing outer surface of the vessel. They are formed from fiberglass-reinforced resins with an interior gel-coat. It is common with above-ground spas for the equipment set (or at least part of it) to be housed inside a small, ventilated step.

The vast majority of home spas, however, are portable, above-ground fiberglass units with self-contained equipment sets concealed by the spa's perimeter skirt. These units range in water capacity from about 100 to more than 1,000 gallons, and are available in a wide variety of shapes.

Typically weighing no more than 500 pounds when empty and requiring a 120- or 240-volt, 20-amp dedicated circuit from your home's electrical service panel (or perhaps from a separate subpanel, depending on the main panel's capacity), portable spas are easy to install and remove. The average portable spa accommodates six adults, and the newer models can be equipped with electronic gadgetry to enhance (or at least modernize) the spa experience.

HOT TUBS

Since their heyday in the 1970s, the deep, cylindrical wooden hot tub remains a sentimental favorite, a rustic alternative to the sleek, contoured, multi-jetted fiberglass spa. Built using the barrel-making craft of coopering, hot tubs remain the vessel of choice for relaxing soaks. Though they can be fitted or built with hydrojets for a spalike experience, purists need only an integral perimeter bench and a heater that can maintain 104° F water temperature.

Hot tubs employ sturdy softwood timber species that are naturally resistant to moisture decay and chemical damage; clear heart, vertical grain, kiln-dried redwood, cypress, cedar, and teak are common hot tub building materials. This wood is used for every component of the tub's construction to ensure a reliable and consistent reaction to the water. But even these woods eventually break down under constant moisture exposure (and certainly water-quality chemicals); given proper care, the expected life span of a new hot tub is about 15 years.

As wooden vessels, hot tubs require a slightly different care and maintenance regimen than fiberglass spas. The wood staves (or vertical side slats) are designed and built to swell in the water, aligning and self-sealing against the metal hoops that contain them; if emptied and left dry longer than two days, the wood will shrink, perhaps never properly or entirely swelling again—and thus leaking—once the tub is refilled.

Preparing (or opening) a new hot tub also takes a bit more time and care than a modern fiberglass or concrete spa, as the wood naturally leaches tannins into the water and leaks or seeps as it swells to watertightness. A hot tub may need to be filled, emptied, and refilled a half-dozen times, and scrubbed with a stiff brush and cleaned each time, before all of the tannins and their remnants are removed and the water can be chemically treated and sanitized.

Traditional wood-built hot tubs are exclusively above-ground vessels; at five feet or more in depth, they are often accessed by a ladder or steps if set on top of a wood deck or patio; more conveniently, they are built into and flush with a deck (or at least partially surrounded by one), providing easier access and a place to cool off between soaks.

A genuine wood hot tub fired by a wood stove is a luxury feature that requires a special setting.

Soft-sided Tubs & Spas ▶

Soft-sided spas with attached or integral jets and filtration systems are a more affordable way to enjoy a relaxing spa experience. Inflatable, collapsible or simply made of non-rigid material, they are smaller than most stay-in-place spas and hot tubs. Still, soft-sided tubs and spas can comfortably accommodate several adults. Typically, they require no extra structural reinforcement below than what a new wood-framed deck or concrete patio slab provides.

The obvious benefit of such spas is their portability. Inflated by a motorized pump or raised up manually and self-supported, soft-sided tubs need only a flat stable surface, a GFCI-protected electrical outlet, and a garden hose to be ready for use.

They are easily and quickly emptied and refilled, but also can be treated with standard chemicals. Some are equipped with heaters; others use an innovative system of recovering or capturing heat from the pump motor to boost the temperature of the spa water, which has several cost and operational benefits. Most manufacturers offer covers that help retain heat, keep debris out of the water, and maintain safety.

Soft-side and inflatable spas generally are intended for on-demand use and aren't designed to be set up on an ongoing basis. This makes them more economical in the long run, but also eliminates the possibility of an impulse soak whenever the motivation hits you.

Pool & Spa Safety

The importance of safety in and around your pool or spa cannot be overstated. Simply, it is your primary responsibility as a pool or spa owner to ensure the safety of everyone who enjoys it, cleans it, keeps the water balanced, or even just peers at it enviously over your privacy fence or self-latching gate.

Comprehensive pool and spa safety encompasses several practical measures. Ideally, your pool or spa was designed and built with safety in mind, including features such as a slip-resistant deck and coping, a secure perimeter fence and gate(s), the proper depth and dimensions for a variety of activities, and provisions for a safety-rated cover.

Other protections recommended by the U.S. Consumer Product Safety Commission (CPSC) to maintain a safe and healthy private swimming pool or spa include: having lifesaving and first aid gear close at hand, properly anchoring handrails and other accessory and accessibility features, and posting easy-to-read signs. A pool or spa safety plan may also include lighting schemes, thermometers (to ensure safe water temperature), and a variety of alarms.

Safety also extends to how and where you store and use the chemicals needed to maintain a healthy water chemistry, as well as setting and enforcing rules of conduct in and around the pool or spa during times when it's open and when it's closed. Carrying an adequate level of homeowner liability insurance—and following the rules to maintain coverage—is a measure of safety as well.

Pools and spas are inherently unsafe, as evidenced by the thousands of unintentional injuries and deaths that the CPSC attributes to the use of private residential swimming pool and spa use every year. But if you approach your ownership responsibility with that understanding and then apply that respect with a variety of measures that lessen the risks and hazards, you'll greatly reduce the chances of experiencing an accident. Building Codes regulating pool and spa construction and installation often dictate these safety-related features, helping explain why the number of private pool and spa injuries and deaths have gone down, even as nearly 800,000 pools and spas are added each year to the several million already in place.

A solid fence on all sides provides privacy for swimming and sunbathing, and it also keeps neighborhood children from venturing into danger. Most local codes require fences or walls around pools and outdoor spas.

Common Safety Practices

A nonskid pool deck is a requirement for a safe swimming area. Broomed concrete is a very popular choice because it is inexpensive and offers great traction even when it's wet.

A sturdy ladder with slip-resistant rungs or steps needs to be well-anchored to provide safe access.

A dome-shaped drain cover keeps objects and limbs from getting drawn into or snagged on the drain.

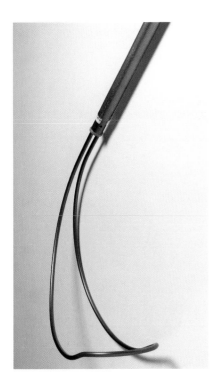

A shepherd's hook with a pole at least 12 ft. long is vital as a tool for reaching a distressed swimmer.

A wood fence near the pool area is a handy spot to mount a waterproof first aid kit.

A self-closing gate latch automatically catches and secures the latch when the gate swings shut.

Party Rules & Safety Tips ▸

Consider these safety tips for a poolside party:

- Put someone in charge of supervising the pool and/ or spa during the party.
- Keep non-swimming activities, including games, cooking and refreshments, and general seating, away from the pool or spa.
- Keep the pool or spa deck free of clutter; store or hang up safety equipment and pool furniture, which can be tripping hazards (especially at night).
- Unless using the pool is part of the party, consider covering it with a reinforced mesh cover so that no one or nothing falls in during the party.

Spa covers not only keep water insulated and prevent evaporation, they are important safety devices that keep children and pets out of danger.

A locking shed or other storage building is much more of a safety requirement than a security requirement. Most pool and spa chemicals are sold in highly concentrated form, making them very dangerous if consumed. DO NOT keep safety and rescue equipment in locked storage.

Signage is an important element of pool and spa safety, especially if you tend to have a lot of guests who may not be familiar with your local rules and preferences. Hang signs in high-visibility spots.

Automatic Pool Covers ▸

Safety-rated automatic pool covers are made from reinforced fabric that can support the weight of several people at a time (although this is not recommended regular usage for the product).

When not in use, the cover is rolled up on a power-driven roller and is stored in a bunker in the pool deck.

Start.

15 seconds.

30 seconds.

Playhouses & Structures

Playhouses and forts are the true domain of children, whether they're located just outside the back door or tucked up into a distant tree.

This chapter shows you how to become the general contractor for your own kid-sized subdivision. A large section on building treehouses explains the techniques you need to know for arboreal building. For the princess or prince in your life, you'll find complete plans for a charming playhouse with a fairy tale spirit. On the less refined, but plenty fun and sturdy, side of things you'll find more compete plans for a log-built fort with a fun bridge and a private clubhouse built over an enclosed play area.

In this chapter:

- Treehouse
- Playhouse
- Log Fort
- Clubhouse

Treehouse

A treehouse is the ultimate un-house. For kids, it's a room that never has to be cleaned. A place for muddy shoes and bug jars and a pocketknife stuck into the wall. A house that you can paint whenever and however you want, without gaining approval. For adults, it's a room that never has to be cleaned, a place for muddy shoes and...well, you get the idea. But best of all a treehouse is up in a tree. And that's just cool.

Let's get started. This chapter walks you through the whole process. First you'll select a tree (or trees). Don't worry if your yard isn't blessed with the perfect specimen; there's help for the arboreally challenged. Moving on to the design phase, you'll consider the options—giving the tree a healthy say—then scratch your head and forge your dreams into a workable plan. Then, after a brief safety lesson, you'll harness up, tie off, and start swinging hammers (not saws). Soon your dream house will be under your feet, or above your head, depending on your position.

A treehouse can look like a miniature, elevated version of a real house, or it can be exotic and fanciful. It can even look like a utility shed in the sky, if that's what you want. But in all cases your treehouse should be safe and fun.

Treehouse Samples

A secret garden in the trees will delight and charm anyone, providing fertile ground for storybook dreams.

A treehouse can become part of a tree. By following the flow of the tree limbs as you design and build, you may find that the tree steers you in intriguing directions.

Treehouses and spaceships often share some design features, contributing to the out-of-this-world appeal of a fort in the trees. Despite appearances, the structure beneath this treehouse is a shed, not an outhouse. (But if it were an outhouse, note that the builder sited it, appropriately, beneath the treehouse, not above it.)

Common house styles can be adapted to your treehouse design with pleasing effect, as with the chalet-inspired treehouse seen here.

Start with a Tree

Finding your host tree is a critical first step in the treehouse planning process. If your host tree isn't up to the task, you'll have to consider a smaller treehouse, or design in some auxiliary posts for structural support.

For most treehouse builders, the tree selection process (and the design selection process that follows) is less of a question of which tree to use than it is an assessment of whether a particular tree is a suitable candidate. While the viability of your structure is the key point, don't neglect to include the health of the tree when making your assessment. You don't want to kill your one beloved tree by burdening it with a structure that is, relative to the lifespan of the tree, temporary.

Many treehouses have been built successfully by incorporating more than one tree into the design. This is usually a good idea from a strength standpoint. However, designing the treehouse can be a lot like working by committee, since trees, like people, tend to act independently when the going gets tough.

Following are some general tips and rules to help you find a suitable host for the treehouse of your dreams. But before you start, there's this advice (it won't be the last time you hear it): When in doubt, ask an arborist. They're in the phone book, they're not expensive, and they can advise you on everything from tree diagnosis to healthy pruning to long term maintenance.

Measure the circumference of any potential host tree to determine if the tree is big enough to support your treehouse. For a normal-size treehouse, a single tree should be at least 5 ft. in circumference at the base.

Building your treehouse in a grouping of trees is a good way to gain adequate support, but it comes with the added challenge of dealing with multiple forces that require some more sophisticated engineering.

How Big Should a Tree Be? ▸

Here are some general guidelines for assessing whether a tree meets minimum size requirements for your treehouse. It is assumed that the tree being considered is mature and healthy and that the treehouse you're planning is a moderately sized (100 square feet or so), single-story structure.

- A single tree that will be the sole support for the house should measure at least five feet in circumference at its base.
- Main supporting limbs (where each limb supports one corner of the house's platform) should be at least six inches in diameter (19-inch circumference).
- Different types and shapes of trees have different strength characteristics—a professional's assessment of your tree can help you plan accordingly.

General Tree Health

A tree doesn't have to be in the absolute prime of its life to be a suitable host for a treehouse, but it must be healthy. Other factors, such as location, can disqualify a candidate as decisively as its general health.

Age. Mature trees are best. They're bigger, stronger, and generally they move less in the wind than younger ones. They also have more heartwood (the hard, inner core of dead wood). When you drive a lag screw into a tree, it's the heartwood that really offers gripping power.

Roots. If your tree's root flares are buried from re-grading or gardening, take it as a warning sign that there might be problems below. Another thing to check for is girdling, where newer roots—often from nearby plants—have grown around the tree's primary anchoring roots, cutting off their life supply. Another warning sign: trees next to unpaved driveways or heavily trodden paths may have suffered damage from all the traffic.

Trunk, branches and leaves (or needles). Inspect the largest members of the tree—the trunk and main branches. Look for large holes and hollow spots, rot on the bark or exposed areas, and signs of bug infestation. Check old wounds and damaged areas to see how the tree is healing. Avoid trees with a significant lean, as they are more likely to topple in a storm. When it comes to branches, look for stout limbs that meet the trunk at a near-perpendicular angle. Typically, the more acute the angle, the weaker the connection, although several suitable tree species naturally have branches set at 45 degrees. Dead branches here and there typically aren't a problem. These should be cut off before you start building. Finally, look at the canopy. In spring and summer the leaves should be green and full with no significant bare spots. Needles on evergreen trees should look normal and healthy.

Straight trunk

Full, green canopy

Root flares (base roots) with natural exposure and no compaction damage

Branches/ Limbs at 90° are strongest

Low, stout limbs or relatively bare trunk

Tree Tips ▶

- When you're building the treehouse and drilling holes for anchor screws, pay attention to the wood chips pulled out by the bit: granulated, dusty material indicates rot inside the tree and should be investigated further. Look for clean spirals and tough flakes or chips.

- Trees with multiple trunks often are fine for building in; however, the trunk junction is vulnerable to being pulled apart, especially under the added stress of a treehouse. The recommended remedy for this is to bind the tree up above with cables to prevent the trunks from spreading. This is a job for an arborist.

- To make sure your tree's foundation stays healthy, don't grow grass or add soil over the root flares. Keep shrubs and other competing plants outside of the ground area defined by the reach of the branches. And by all means, keep cars and crowds off the base roots, especially on trees with shallow root systems.

Planning

If you built a treehouse as a kid you probably didn't spend a lot of time planning it beforehand. You had plenty of ideas and knew what you wanted—a trap door, a lookout post, a tire swing, and maybe a parachuting platform or helicopter pad—you just weren't exactly sure how everything would come together. In the end, you decided to figure it out along the way and got started.

Of course, some people might use the same approach today (good luck on the helicopter pad), but be advised that a little planning up front could save your project from disaster. Remember the guy with the metal clipboard from the city office? You don't want him showing up with a demolition order just as you're nailing up the last piece of trim.

Take time at the beginning of your project to address some basics, including general design features such as the size and style of the treehouse, where it will sit in the tree, and how you'll get from the ground to the front door—if you want a front door. *Note: Before refining your treehouse plans, read the remainder of this section for important safety-related design considerations.*

Planning your treehouse can be as much fun as building it, or even using it, if you choose to involve everyone and make it into a teaching/learning experience. After all, you're never too young to learn about Building Codes and zoning laws.

Building Codes & Zoning Laws

When it comes to Building Codes and treehouses, the official word is that there is no official word. Many municipalities—the governing powers over building and zoning laws—consider treehouses to be "temporary" structures when they fit within certain size limits, typically about 100 to 120 square feet and not more than 10 to 12 feet tall. If you have concerns about the restrictiveness of the local laws, keeping your treehouse within their size limits for temporary structures is a good precaution to take.

Drafting a set of standards for structures built on living, moving, and infinitely variable foundations (trees) quickly becomes a cat-herding exercise for engineers. Thus, few codes exist that set construction standards for treehouses. This means more responsibility is placed on the builder.

When it comes to zoning laws, the city planning office is concerned less with a treehouse's construction and more with its impact on your property. They may state that you can't build anything within three feet or more of your property line (called setback restriction) or that you can't build a treehouse in your front yard (the Joneses might not be the treehouse type).

The bottom line is this: Your local planning office might require you to get a building permit and pass inspections for your treehouse, or they might not care what you do, provided you keep the building within specific parameters. It's up to you to learn the rules. Although city laws are all over the map regarding treehouses, here are a few common-sense tips that are worth following no matter where you live:

- Talk with your neighbors about your treehouse plans. A show of respect and diplomacy on your part is likely to prevent them from filing a complaint with the authorities.
- Use discretion when selecting locations for windows (and decks) in your treehouse. Your neighbors might be a touch uncomfortable if you suddenly have a commanding view of their hot tub or a straight shot into their second-story windows.
- Electrical and plumbing service running to a treehouse tells the authorities that you plan to live there, thus your house crosses a big line from "temporary structure" to "residence" or "dwelling" and becomes subject to all the requirements of the standard building code.
- Don't build in a frontyard tree or other locations that are easily viewed from a public road.

The point is not to hide from the authorities, it's that conspicuous treehouses attract too much attention and curiosity for the city's comfort, and the house might annoy your neighbors.

- In addition to keeping the size of your treehouse reasonable, pay attention to any height restriction for backyard structures. Treehouses can easily exceed these, for obvious reasons, but nevertheless may be held to the same height limits as sheds, garages, and other types of buildings.
- Even if the local building laws don't cover treehouses, you can look to the regular Building Code for guidance. It outlines construction standards for things like railings, floor joist spans, and accommodations for local weather and geologic (earthquake) conditions.

Family DIY ▸

If you're building a treehouse for kids to use or share with the adults, include them in the design process. Many a parent has gone to great lengths to surprise kids with a fancy treehouse that ultimately doesn't get used. Not only will kids get more pleasure from a house they help to create, but by finding practical solutions to bring their creative ideas to life, they also will learn the essence of architecture. Who knows, you might have another Frank Lloyd Wright on your hands, or better yet for treehouses, another Christopher Wren.

Treehouse Safety

The fact is, a house up in a tree comes with some risks. But so does an elevated deck off of your kitchen or a jungle gym in your backyard. What makes you comfortable using any part of your house on a daily basis is your knowledge that it was designed thoughtfully to prevent common hazards. Performing conscientious, regular maintenance of a treehouse, or any other structure, ensures its safety and helps protect your peace of mind. The same applies to treehouses, although treehouses present an additional safety consideration—building off the ground.

Treehouse safety can be divided into two categories: safe design and safe working conditions. Both are equally important and perfectly manageable, and both should be followed regardless of who uses the house. A kids' treehouse naturally involves more safety concerns than one used exclusively by adults. However, keep in mind that you never know when children might visit, and it's too late once they're up there. It's like bringing a two-year-old into a non-baby-proofed home. The adults are suddenly scrambling madly as they discover all the things that are perfectly safe for them but potentially deadly for a toddler.

A safe design and safe building practices are essential to a successful treehouse project. Building a backyard structure is a great chance to involve kids and show them the right way to work with tools.

Safe Treehouse Design

The primary safeguard on any treehouse is the supporting platform. It alone keeps the house and its occupants aloft. Even if every other element is designed to the highest standards, a treehouse is completely unsafe if the platform isn't sound. Later information covers platform construction in detail, so for now, just two quick reminders:

1. Build platforms for kids' treehouses no higher than eight feet above the ground.
2. Inspect the platform support members and tree connections regularly to make sure everything's in good shape.

With a strong, stable platform in place, you can turn your attention to the other elements of safety in design.

Everything's riding on the treehouse platform. Be sure to keep it in good condition.

Sound, code-compliant railings are a critical safety feature for treehouse users of all ages.

RAILINGS

Every part of a treehouse platform that isn't bound by walls must have a sturdy railing. Building codes around the country tend to agree on railing specifications, and these are the best rules to follow for treehouses, too.

In general, railings must be at least 36" tall, with vertical balusters no more than 4" apart. A railing should be strong enough to withstand several adults leaning against it at once, as well as roughhousing kids. On treehouses for small children, use only standard 2 × 2 lumber or other rigid vertical balusters, not rope or cable balusters. For kids of all ages, don't use horizontal balusters. These work well for cattle fencing, but kids are too tempted to climb them. See page 201 for more railing specifications and instructions on building railings.

ACCESS LANDINGS

Each type of access to a treehouse—ladder, rope, stairs, etc.—has its own design standards for safety, but all must have a landing point for arriving and departing. In many cases, the landing necessitates a gap in a railing or other opening and thus a potential fall hazard. Keep this in mind when planning access to your treehouse, and consider these recommendations:

- Include a safety rail across openings in railings (this is a must, not an option).
- Leave plenty of room around access openings, enough for anyone to safely climb onto the treehouse platform and stand up without backing up.
- Consider non-slip decking on landings to prevent falls if the surface gets wet.
- Add handles at the sides of access openings and anywhere else to facilitate climbing up and down; handholds cut into the treehouse floor work well, too.
- Install a safety gate to bar young children from areas where there are access openings.

A sturdy handle is a welcome sight to tired climbers. Make sure all handles and mounting hardware are galvanized or otherwise corrosion-protected.

WINDOWS & DOORS

The obvious safety hazard for windows and doors is glass. So the rule is: Don't use it, especially in kids' treehouses. Standard glass is too easily broken during play or by swaying branches or rocks thrown by taunted older brothers. Instead, use strong plastic sheeting. The strongest stuff is ¼"-thick polycarbonate glazing. It's rated for outdoor public buildings, like kiosks and bus stops, so it can easily survive the abuse from your own little vandals. Plastic does get scratched and some becomes cloudy over time, but it's easily replaceable and is better than a trip to the emergency room.

Even more important than the glazing is the placement of doors and windows. All doors and operable windows must open over a deck, not a drop to the ground. If a door is close to an access point, make sure there's ample floor space between the door and any opening in a railing, for example.

GROUND BELOW THE TREE

Since occasional short falls are likely to occur when kids are climbing around trees, it's a good idea to fill the area beneath your treehouse with a soft ground cover. The best material for the health of the tree is wood chips. A 6"-thick bed of wood chips effectively cushions a fall from 7 feet, according to the National Resource Center for Health and Safety in Child Care. Also, keep the general area beneath the house free of rocks, branches, and anything else one would prefer not to land on.

A soft bed of loose ground cover is recommended under any kids' treehouse or areas where kids will be climbing.

Treefort Knox ▸

Locking up may seem unnecessary for most backyard hideaways, but for some treehouses it's a sensible precaution. For example, treehouses located out of your daily view, especially those near a public road, can attract a lot of negative attention, like vandalism. More importantly, kids just can't resist getting into stuff, and you don't want to face a lawsuit because you made it easy for them to waltz into your house and get hurt. Of course, you had nothing to do with it. But try telling that to a plaintiff lawyer.

These are just suggestions, not legal advice:

- Install a strong door with a padlock (¾" plywood backed by a lumber frame is a good choice; it may be ugly, but it's strong).
- Post signage stating "No Trespassing," "Private Property," "Danger," or similar warnings.
- Install window shutters that lock on the inside or can be padlocked from the outside.
- Use plastic instead of glass in windows (the polycarbonate glazing mentioned on page 187 won't be broken with rocks).
- Use a retractable or removable ladder as the only means of access, and take it away when you leave the treehouse.

CONSTRUCTION DETAILS

One of the first rules of building children's play structures is to countersink all exposed fasteners. For good reason. If you fall and slide along a post, you might get a scrape and some splinters, but you're much better off than if your kneecap hits a protruding bolt on the way down. Follow the countersink rule for all kids' treehouses.

Speaking of splinters, take the time to sand rough edges as you build your house. Your kids and guests will be glad you did. Also keep an eye out for sharp points, protruding nails, and any rusty metal.

MAINTENANCE

Treehouses fight a constant battle with gravity. This, combined with outdoor exposure and the threat of rust and rot make regular inspections of the house a critical safety precaution. Inspect your treehouse several times throughout the year for signs of rot or damage to structural members and all supporting hardware. Also check everything after big storms and high winds, as excessive tree movement can easily cause damage to wood structures or break anchors without you

knowing it. Test safety railings, handholds, and access equipment more frequently.

Inspect the tree around connecting points for stress fractures and damage to the bark. Weighted members and tensioned cables and ropes rubbing against the bark can be deadly for a tree if it cuts into the layers just below the bark. Check openings where the trunk and branches pass through the treehouse, and expand them as needed to avoid strangling the tree. Finally, remove dead or damaged branches that could fall on the house.

Neglected support beams and connections are the most common causes of treehouse disasters. Check these parts often for rot, corrosion, and damage and replace immediately if evidence is found.

Working Safely

Off-the-ground work has its own long list of safety guidelines on top of the regular set of basic construction safety rules. Since you can learn about general tool and job site safety anywhere (please do so), the focus here is on matters specific to treehouse building and related gravity-defying feats. But here are some good points to keep in mind.

Working outdoors presents challenges not faced in the interior, such as dealing with the weather, working at heights, and staying clear of power lines. By taking a few common-sense safety precautions, you can perform exterior work safely.

Dress appropriately for the job and weather. Avoid working in extreme temperatures, hot or cold, and never work outdoors during a storm or high winds.

Work with a helper whenever possible—especially when working at heights. If you must work alone, tell a family member or friend so the person can check in with you periodically. If you own a cell phone, keep it with you at all times.

Don't use tools or work at heights after consuming alcohol. If you're taking medicine, read the label and follow the recommendations regarding the use of tools and equipment.

When using ladders, extend the top of the ladder three feet above the roof edge for greater stability. Climb on and off the ladder at a point as close to the ground as possible. Use caution and keep your center of gravity low when moving from a ladder onto a roof. Keep your hips between the side rails when reaching over the side of a ladder, and be careful not to extend yourself too far or it could throw off your balance. Move the ladder as often as necessary to avoid overreaching. Finally, don't exceed the work-load rating for your ladder. Read and follow the load limits and safety instructions listed on the label.

HARDHAT AREA (HEADS UP!)

The general area underneath the tree should be off limits to anyone not actively working on the project at hand. Someone walking idly underneath to check things out might not be engaged enough to react if something falls. Hardhats are a good idea for anyone working on the project and for kids anywhere close to the job site.

To keep an extension cord from dropping—and sometimes taking your tool with it—wrap the cord around a branch to carry the bulk of the weight. Also, wear a tool belt to keep tools and fasteners within reach while keeping your hands free to grab lumber, etc.

During construction, ladder management is an exceptionally important aspect of jobsite safety. Since trees generally do not afford flat, smooth areas for the ladder rungs to rest, adding padded tips will help stabilize the ladder. And remember: a fall of just a couple of feet from a ladder can cause a fractured elbow or worse.

PULLEY SYSTEMS

A pulley is one of the fun features found on a lot of treehouses. They're great for delivering baskets full of food and supplies. During the build, a simple pulley set up with a bucket or crate is handy for hauling up tools and hardware.

Here's an easy way to set up a simple, lightweight pulley:

1. Using a strong nylon or hemp rope (don't use polypropylene, which doesn't stand up under sun exposure), tie one end to a small sandbag and throw it over a strong branch.
2. Tie a corrosion-resistant pulley near the end of the rope, then tie a loop closer to the end, using bowline knots for both.
3. Feed a second rope through the pulley and temporarily secure both ends so the rope won't slip through the pulley.
4. Thread the first rope through the loop made in step 2, then haul the pulley up snug to the branch. Tie off the end you're holding to secure the pulley to the branch.

For heavy-duty lifting, use a block and tackle, which is a pulley system that has one rope strung through two sets of pulleys (blocks). The magic of multiple-pulley systems is that the lifting power is increased by 1× for each pulley. For example, a block and tackle with 6 pulleys gives you 6 pounds of lifting force for each pound of force you put onto the pulling rope. If you weigh 150 pounds and hang on the pulling end, you could raise a nearly 900 lb. load without moving a muscle. The drawback is that you have to pull the rope six times farther than if you were using a single pulley. For a high treehouse, you'll need a lot of rope.

When hauling up loads with a block and tackle, try to have a second person on the ground to man a control line tied to the load. This helps stabilize the load and steer it through branches and other obstacles. Additional control like this makes it safer for those up in the tree.

A block and tackle makes it easy to lift heavy support beams and pre-built walls.

Safety Checklists ▶

SAFE DESIGN CHECKLIST

- Platform no more than 8 ft. above ground (for kids' treehouse).
- Strong railings 36" high, with balusters no more than 4" apart.
- Continuous railing along all open decks and at sides of stairs.
- Safety rail across all access openings.
- No horizontal railing balusters.
- Large access landings with handles or handholds as needed.
- No ladder rungs nailed to tree (see page 192).
- Non-slip decking around access openings.
- No glass windows in kids' treehouses.
- Doors and operable windows open onto a deck, not a drop.
- Soft ground cover beneath kids' treehouses.
- Fasteners countersunk in all exposed areas.
- No rough wood edges, sharp points, or protruding nails or screws.
- Screws and bolts only for structural connections to tree; no nails.
- Regular maintenance check of platform support members and tree connections, railings, access equipment, and handles.
- Refer to local building codes for your area.

SAFE CONSTRUCTION CHECKLIST

- Safety ropes and harness for any high work.
- Tie onto safety line even after platform is complete.
- No kids or visitors under tree during construction.
- Hardhats for workers on ground and all kids.
- Follow basic construction safety and ladder safety rules.

Building Platforms

It's time to get this house off the ground. The platform is the first and most important part of the building process. It also tends to be the most challenging, so unfortunately there's no warming up on the easy stuff. Do a good job here and for the rest of the project you'll have the satisfaction of knowing your house will be safe, secure, and level.

To build a proper platform, you'll need to determine what types of anchors will hold up best against the host tree's natural movement throughout the year. You'll also decide on sizing for support beams and floor framing, based on the size of your house and how much it will weigh (don't worry, you won't have to stand on a scale with each 2 × 4). As before, the tree should be your primary guide.

This chapter walks you through some basics of platform construction, the main types of anchors for support beams, and installation of the floor decking. You'll then get a construction overview of platforms for several popular treehouse configurations. Please keep in mind that all methods and configurations shown here are merely drawn from examples that have worked on other treehouses. On your own treehouse, you alone are the architect, engineer, and builder, and it's up to you to determine what is suitable for your situation. If you have any concerns about the structural viability of your platform or the health of your tree, consult a qualified building professional or arborist.

The treehouse platform needs to be solidly constructed, square, level and (above all) securely attached to the tree or trees.

Platform Basics

A typical treehouse platform is made up of support beams and a floor frame. The beams are anchored to the tree and carry the weight of the entire structure. The frame is made up of floor joists that run perpendicular to the beams. Topped with decking, the floor frame becomes the finished floor of the treehouse, onto which you build the walls and everything thereafter. Some small kids' treehouses have only a floor as the supporting structure, particularly when the house is low to the ground and is well-supported by branches.

Sizing beams and floor joists isn't an exact science, as it is with a regular house, but standard span tables can give you an idea about load limits for your treehouse. Contact your local building department for span tables and materials requirements for beams (also called girders), floor joists, and decking materials. What's unique to treehouses is the additional stress of the tree's motion and possible twisting forces applied to the floor frame. Flexible anchors are the best defense against tree motion, as you'll see later. In any case, it's better to err on the side of oversized support members.

The trick to building a successful platform is not just in the strength and stability. The platform must also be level. If you've ever been in an old house with a sloping floor, you know why. It messes with your sense of equilibrium and gives you an uneasy "funhouse" feeling. In a treehouse this can lead to a perceived sense of instability, plus it gives your friends and family something to make fun of. One handy technique for locating anchor points to create a level platform is to set up a mason's string and line level.

A few more tips for building platforms:

- Use a single ¾"-dia. galvanized lag screw to anchor lumber directly to the tree. For lightweight supports, you can get away with ½" lag screws, but don't use anything smaller.
- If a situation calls for more than one screw in any part of the tree, never place two screws in a vertical line less than 12" apart. To the tree, each screw is treated as a wound; if the screws are too close together, the wounds might coalesce, causing the area to rot.
- Never remove bark to create a flat surface for anchoring, etc. If done carefully, it's okay to shave the surface slightly, but always leave the protective layer of bark intact. A better solution is to use wood wedges to level out brackets and other anchors.
- When you're building a platform up in the tree, it's often helpful to cut beams or joists long at first, allowing some play as you piece the frame together. Cut off the excess after the framing is completed, or leave beam ends long to use as outriggers for pulleys, swings, etc.

Fasteners placed close together in a vertical line can lead to rot in the tree, causing the anchors to fail.

Platform Anchoring Techniques

Anchoring the platform is all about dealing with tree movement. Here's the problem: If you're building in or around a section of the tree that's used to moving a lot in the wind and you tie multiple parts of the tree (or parts of different trees) together, something's got to give. Usually it's your platform's support beams or anchors that lose the battle by breaking or simply shearing off. The best solution is to respect Mother Nature by using anchors that make allowances for movement.

Treehouse builders have come up with a range of anchoring methods for different situations, but most fall into one of the four categories shown here. Knowing the main types of anchors will help you decide what's best for your project. Often a combination of different anchors is the most effective approach.

FIXED ANCHOR

A fixed anchor is the most basic type, with the support beams firmly anchored to the tree with large lag screws. Because they allow for zero tree movement, fixed anchors are typically used on single-tree houses anchored exclusively to the trunk, or perhaps used in conjunction with a flexible anchor (sliding or hanging—see page 194) at the opposite end of the beam.

To install a fixed anchor, drill a slightly oversized hole for a lag screw through the beam, just below the center of the beam's depth. Drill a pilot hole into the tree that's slightly smaller than the screw's shank. Add one washer on the outside of the beam and one or two large, thick washers on the tree side, and anchor the beam to the tree with the lag screw. The washers on the tree side of the beam help prevent chafing of the beam against the bark.

Sizing the screw: Use a ¾" galvanized lag screw that's long enough to penetrate at least 5" to 6" into the tree's solid wood. Accounting for a 2× (1½"-thick) beam, the washers, and the bark, you need at least a 9" screw for a major beam connection.

Centerline of beam

Centerline of screw hole

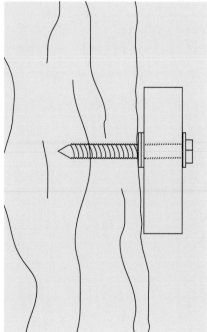

A single lag screw is an adequate fixed anchor for a beam, provided the screw is heavy enough. Multiple screws can cause damage to your tree. Thread a washer between the screw head and the beam, and add at least a couple washers between the beam and the tree to prevent the beam from rubbing against and damaging the bark.

A slot-type sliding anchor allows single-directional movement between the tree or trees and the platform beams.

A bracket-type sliding anchor allows two-directional movement while offering solid support. Unfortunately, you'll have to have these custom-fabricated at a local metal shop.

A screw eye or through bolt hanging anchor requires a tree limb at least 6" in diameter.

Knee braces support the platform, distributing the load onto the trunk and off of the lag screws that attach the beams to the tree trunk.

Platform Designs

A single-tree platform nestled in tree branches has a sturdy floor frame made from 2 × 6s and anchored directly to the tree.

Single tree with trunk as center post has a joist frame that rests on a pair of parallel supports that are bolted to the trunk. Braces running from the outer frame joists to the tree trunk stabilize the frame.

A platform spanning two tree trunks is supported by parallel 2 × 10 beams that are attached to both trunks. V-braces stabilize the outside joist frame members.

Two trees and two support posts give direct support to every corner of the treehouse platform. Posts should be set on a concrete pier that extends below the frostline.

Installing Decking

If you're thinking that you've just jumped from platform beams to decking and skipped the floor framing, you're right. Because the configuration of the floor framing tends to follow the platform design, you'll get a better picture of that with the individual platform overviews on page 195.

Most treehouse platforms are decked using standard decking techniques. It's a lot like decking a… well, a deck, or a floor, depending on the materials used. Standard decking materials include ⁵⁄₄ × 6 decking boards, 2 × 6 lumber, and ¾" exterior-grade plywood. Of these, plywood is the cheapest and easiest to install, but it comes with one drawback: Treehouse floors tend to get wet, and the water has no place to go on a solid plywood surface. By contrast, decking boards can—and should—be gapped to allow water through and eliminate pooling. If you're really committed to creating a dry interior on your house,

you might consider plywood or tongue-and-groove decking boards, which make a smooth, strong floor without gaps.

Install decking boards with deck screws driven through pilot holes (although you would normally nail tongue-and-groove boards). Use screws that are long enough to penetrate the floor framing by at least 1¼". Gap the boards ¼" apart, or more, if desired. Two screws at each joist are sufficient. Install plywood decking with 2" deck screws, driven every 6" along the perimeter and every 8" in the field of the sheet.

To allow for tree growth, try to leave a 2" gap between the decking and the tree. This means you'll have to scribe the decking and cut it to fit around tree penetrations. To scribe a board, set it on the floor as close as possible to its final position, then use a compass to trace the contours of the tree onto the board.

Fasten the decking to the floor frame with corrosion-resistant deck screws. Below: Use a compass to scribe decking boards at tree penetrations.

2" gap

Framing Walls

In the interest of making friends with gravity, treehouse walls are typically framed with 2 × 2 or 2 × 3 lumber, as opposed to the standard 2 × 4 or 2 × 6 framing used in traditional houses. Single-story treehouses can usually get away with 24" on-center stud spacing instead of the standard 16" spacing. However, the siding you use may determine the spacing, as some siding requires support every 16".

How tall you build the walls is up to you. Standard wall height is 8 ft. Treehouses have no standard, of course, but 6- ft. to 7 ft. gives most people enough headroom while maintaining a more intimate scale appropriate for a hideaway. Another consideration is wall shape. Often two of the four walls follow the shape of the roof, while the two adjacent walls are level across the top. Building wall shapes other than the rectangle or square are discussed later.

BASIC WALL CONSTRUCTION

A wall frame has horizontal top and bottom plates fastened over the ends of vertical studs. Where a window is present, a horizontal sill and header are installed between two studs to create a rough opening (door rough openings have only a header, along the top). On treehouses, similar framed openings can be used to frame around large tree penetrations.

In a four-walled structure, two of the walls are known as "through" walls and two are "butt" walls. The only difference is that through walls overlap the ends of the butt walls and are made longer to compensate for the thickness of the butt walls. For simplicity, the two through walls and two butt walls oppose each other so that both members of each type are made the same length.

Build stud walls on the ground and then lift them up onto the platform one wall at a time. Below: Through walls overlap butt walls and are fastened together to form a corner of the house.

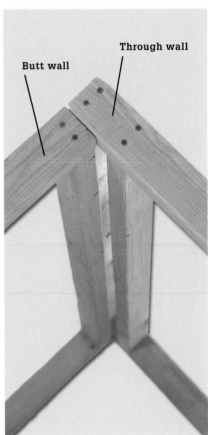

Through wall

Butt wall

Assemble the wall frame with screws or nails. Add short cripple studs to continue the general stud layout at window and door openings.

To build a wall frame, cut the top and bottom plates to equal the total wall length (not counting the siding and trim). Lay the plates together on the ground—or driveway or garage floor—with their ends even. Mark the stud layout onto the plates, using 16" or 24" on-center spacing. Mark for an extra stud at each side of window and door openings; these are in addition to, and should not interrupt, the general stud layout. If you plan to install interior paneling or other finish, add an extra end stud to each end of the through walls. This gives you something to nail to when the walls are fitted together. Extra studs might also come in handy for nailing exterior siding.

Cut the studs to equal the total wall height minus 3", the combined thickness of the plates. Position the plates over the ends of the studs, and fasten them with two 3" galvanized wood screws or deck screws driven through pilot holes. You can screw through the plates into the ends of the studs, or angle the screws

(toenail) through opposing sides of the studs and into the plates. You can also use 10d or 16d galvanized nails instead of screws.

To frame a window opening, measure up from the bottom of the bottom plate, and mark the sill and header heights onto both side studs. *Note: If you're using a homemade window, make the rough opening 1½" wider and 2¼" taller than the finished (glazed) window dimensions.* This accounts for the window jambs made from ¾"-thick lumber and a sill made from 2 × 4 lumber. If you're using a recycled window sash (without its own frame), make the rough opening 1¾" wider and 2½" taller than the sash. Cut the sill and header and install them between the side studs, making sure the rough opening is perfectly square. Install short cripple studs below the sill and above the header to complete the general stud layout. Follow the same procedure to frame a rough opening for a door, making it 2½" wider and 1¼" taller than the finished door opening (for a homemade door).

FRAMING OTHER WALL SHAPES

If you're going with a gable or shed roof for your treehouse, frame the two end walls to follow the roof slope. This not only encloses the walls up to the roof, it also establishes the roofline so you have an easy starting point for framing the roof. Houses with hip roofs have four standard walls—with horizontal top plates. Curved walls (for conical roofs) are also flat across the top but are framed a little differently than standard walls.

To frame an end wall for a gable or shed roof:

First determine the roof's slope. In builders' parlance, roof slope, or pitch, is expressed in a rise-run ratio. For example, a 6-in-12 roof rises 6" for every 12" of horizontal run, equivalent to an angle of about 26.5°. A 12-in-12 roof slopes at 45°. For most do-it-yourselfers, it's easier to determine the roof slope using only the angle. Another trick to simplify roof framing is to lay out the entire outline of the wall by snapping chalk lines onto a garage floor or mat of plywood sheets. Then you can simply measure to your lines to find the lengths of the pieces.

For a gable end wall, let's say the roof slope is 30° (that's a little flatter than a 7-in-12 pitch). That means the top ends of all the studs, as well as the top ends of the two top plates, are cut at 30°. Snap a chalk line to represent the bottom of the wall, then snap two lines perpendicular to the first representing the ends of the wall. *Note: The gable end wall must be a through wall.* Measure up from the bottom line and mark the side lines at the total wall height; this is equal to the total height of the side (non-sloping) walls.

Now make a center line running up through the middle of the wall layout. Cut one end of each of the two top plates at 30°, leaving the other ends long for now. Set the angled ends of the plates together so they meet on the center line and each plate also intersects one of the top-of-wall marks on a side line. See your wall now? You can trace along the undersides of the top plates, or just leave them in place, then measure up from the bottom line to find the lengths of all the studs—remember to take off 1½" from the stud lengths to account for the bottom plate. Cut the top plates to length so their bottom ends will be flush with the outside faces of the side walls.

To lay out an end wall for a shed roof—let's say at 15°—snap a bottom chalk line and two perpendicular side lines, as with the gable end wall. The end walls for a shed roof must also be through walls. Mark the wall heights onto the side lines. Snap a chalk line between those two marks, and your layout is done. All of the top ends of the studs are cut at 15°.

Gable end wall layout with 30° roof pitch.

Shed end wall layout with 15° roof pitch.

FRAMING CURVED WALLS

Structurally, curved walls are essentially the same as standard walls. They have top and bottom plates, studs, and similar rough openings for windows and doors. The main difference, and the trick to making the curve, is in using a double layer of ¾" plywood for each of the plates. Also, the stud spacing is set according to the exterior siding material. Use 2 × 3 or larger studs for framing curved walls.

Lay out curved wall plates using a trammel: a thin, flat board with a pivot nail near one end and two holes for a pencil near the other end. Space the pencil holes to match the width (depth) of the wall's studs. The distances between the pencil holes and the pivot nail determine the inner and outer radii of the curve. Mark the plate outlines onto full or partial sheets of ¾" exterior-grade plywood, and make the cuts with a jigsaw. You can piece together the plates as needed to minimize waste.

Space the studs according to the siding you'll use: For plywood, space the studs 2" for every 12" of outside radius on the curve—a 36" radius gets studs every 6". For other types of siding, such as vertical 1 × 4 tongue-&-groove boards, lay out the studs at 24" on center, then install 2× nailers horizontally between the studs along the midpoint of the wall. The nailers must be cut with the same radius as the wall plates.

Use a trammel to mark the cutting lines for curved wall plates, pivoting the trammel from a centerpoint.

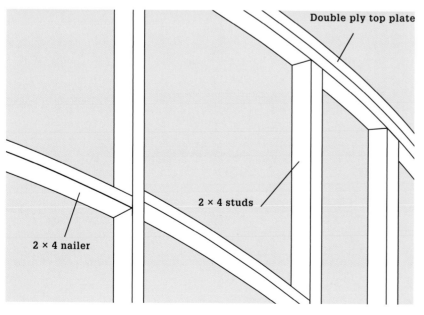

Double ply top plate

2 × 4 studs

2 × 4 nailer

Install 2× nailers between studs for vertical siding. Stagger the nailers up and down to allow room for fastening.

Building Railings

A railing is primarily a safety device. All too often, amateur and even professional designers (especially professional designers) see railings as an opportunity to get creative. The result is an unsuitable railing, which is essentially useless. Build a strong, solid railing with closely spaced balusters and you won't have to worry about who uses the treehouse, whether it's small children or tipsy adults. That means no ropes, no cables, and no twigs. Okay. Lecture over.

A good treehouse railing employs the basic construction details of a standard deck railing. Many treehouse railings are even simpler, eliminating features like the broad horizontal cap rail commonly found on house decks. The important thing is to adhere to the following basic design requirements:

- Tops of railings must be at least 36" above the platform surface.
- Balusters (vertical spindles) may be spaced no more than 4" apart.
- Horizontal balusters are unsafe for children, who like to climb them.
- Railing posts (4 × 4 or larger lumber) may be spaced no more than 6 ft. apart and must be anchored to the platform frame, not the decking.

- Top and bottom rails should be installed on the inside faces of railing posts.
- Balusters should be fastened with screws; if nails are used, balusters must be on the inside of horizontal rails.
- All openings in railings—for access to the treehouse platform—must have a safety rail across the top.

To build a simple railing, cut 4 × 4 support posts to extend from the bottom edge (or close to the edge) of the platform's floor joists to 36" above the decking surface. Anchor the posts on the outside of the joists with pairs of ½" carriage bolts with washers. Install posts at the ends of railing runs and every 6 ft. in between, and at both sides of access openings and stairways.

Cut 2 × 4 or 2 × 6 horizontal rails to span between the top ends of the posts. Fasten the rails to the inside faces of the posts with pairs of 3" deck screws. Continue the rail through access openings to create a safety barrier. Mark the baluster layout onto the outside faces of the rails, spacing the balusters no more than 4" apart. Cut 2 × 2 balusters to extend from the top of the rail down to the floor framing, overlapping the joists by at least 4". Fasten the balusters to the rails and joists with pairs of 2½" deck screws driven into pilot holes at each end.

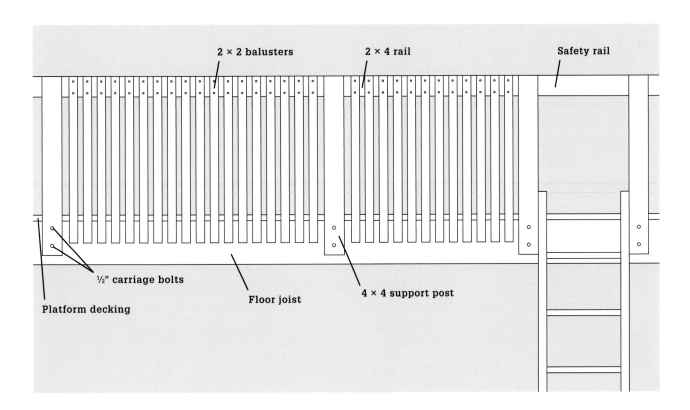

Building Roofs

A treehouse roof is constructed just as any other small outbuilding roof, with the possible exception of the tree trunk that may project through it. If you are not experienced with building and covering roofs, consult an additional source for further information

If you framed your walls with extreme care and everything came out square and perfectly level, you could design your roof frame on paper and use mathematical calculations to find all the angles and locate the necessary cuts. But because you're building in a tree, you're likely to have a better chance at success framing your roof using a cut-to-fit approach. The main structural members of any framed roof are the rafters and the roof deck, which is usually made from plywood roof sheathing.

On a gable roof, the rafters sit on top of the sidewalls and meet at a ridge board, or ridge beam, at the roof's peak. Rafters on hip roofs also form a peak, meeting at a ridge beam, or more commonly in treehouses, at the tree's trunk. A shed roof has no peak, and the rafters simply span from wall to wall. A roof's overall strength is determined primarily by the size of rafters and how closely they're spaced. Because treehouses tend to be small buildings, their roofs are typically built with 2 × 3 or 2 × 4 rafters spaced 16 or 24 inches on center. Check with the local building department for rafter span recommendations for your area.

Choose a roofing material for the roof deck, or sheathing. If you're building a small treehouse, take the easy route and use plywood. On any house with a gable or shed roof, consider adding 1x trim up against the underside of the roof sheathing along the end walls, to hide the faces of the outer rafters. For roofcoverings, your principal choices are asphalt shingles, cedar shingles, or metal roof panels.

A shed roof is the easiest to build among permanent roofs. It can be covered with just about any material, including shingles, roll roofing and roof panels.

Treehouse Roof Options

Gable roofs are considered the most classic roof style, with angled wall sections at either end.

A removable roof made from canvas or a plastic tarp may be all you need to shelter a tree fort or sun deck.

Hip roofs are sloped on all sides and are more difficult to frame than sheds and gables.

A conical roof is an impressive way to top a rounded wall. They're built with closely spaced rafters fanning out from the roof peak.

Playhouse

Playhouses are all about stirring the imagination. Loaded with fancy American Gothic details, this charming little house makes a special play home for kids and an attractive backyard feature for adults. In addition to its architectural character (see Gothic Style, below), what makes this a great playhouse design is its size—the enclosed house measures 5 × 7½ ft. and includes a 5-ft.-tall door and plenty of headroom inside. This means your kids will likely "outgrow" the playhouse before they get too big for it. And you can always give the house a second life as a storage shed.

At the front of the house is a 30"-deep porch complete with real decking boards and a nicely decorated railing. Each side wall features a window and flower box, and the "foundation" has the look of stone created by wood blocks applied to the floor framing. All of these features are optional, but each one adds to the charm of this well-appointed playhouse.

As shown here, the floor of the playhouse is anchored to four 4 × 4 posts buried in the ground.

As an alternative, you can set the playhouse on 4 × 6 timber skids. Another custom variation you might consider is in the styling of the verge boards (the gingerbread gable trim). Instead of using the provided pattern, you can create a cardboard template of your own design. Architectural plan and pattern books from the Gothic period are full of inspiration for decorative ideas.

Gothic Style ▸

The architectural style known as American Gothic (also called Gothic Revival and Carpenter Gothic) dates back to the 1830s and essentially marks the beginning of the Victorian period in American home design. Adapted from a similar movement in England, Gothic style was inspired by the ornately decorated stone cathedrals found throughout Europe. The style quickly evolved in America as thrifty carpenters learned to re-create and reinterpret the original decorative motifs using wood instead of stone.

American Gothic's most characteristic feature is the steeply pitched roof with fancy scroll-cut bargeboards, or verge boards, which gave the style its popular nickname, "gingerbread." Other typical features found on Gothic homes (and the Gothic Playhouse) include board-and-batten siding, doors and windows shaped with Gothic arches, and spires or finials adorning roof peaks.

Materials List

Description	No./Size	Material
Foundation/Floor		
Drainage material	1 cu. yd.	Compactable gravel
Foundation posts	(4) Field measure	4 × 4 pressure-treated landscape timbers
Concrete	Field measure	3,000 psi concrete
Rim joists	(3) 10', (1) 8'	2 × 12 pressure-treated, rated for ground contact
Floor joists	(1) 10', (2) 8'	2 × 6 pressure-treated
Box sills (rim joists)	(2) 12'	2 × 4 pressure-treated
Floor sheathing	(2) 4 × 8' sheets	¾" ext.-grade plywood
Porch decking	(5) 10'	1 × 6 pressure-treated decking
Foundation "stones"	(7) 10'	⁵⁄₄ × 6" treated decking w/radius edge (R.E.D.), rated for ground contact
Framing		
Wall framing & railings	(29) 12'	2 × 4
Rafters & spacers	(7) 12'	2 × 4
Ridge board	(1) 8'	1 × 6
Collar ties	(1) 10'	1 × 4
Exterior Finishes		
Siding, window boxes & door trim	(26) 10'	1 × 8 pressure-treated or cedar
Battens & trim	(30) 8'	1 × 2 pressure-treated or cedar
Door panel, verge boards & fascia	(10) 10'	1 × 6 pressure-treated or cedar
Door braces, trim & railing trim	(2) 10'	1 × 4 pressure-treated or cedar
Railing posts	(2) 8'	4 × 4 pressure-treated
Railing balusters	(4) 8'	2 × 2 pressure-treated or cedar
Window stops	(2) 8'	³⁄₈" pressure-treated or cedar quarter-round molding
Window glazing (optional)	(4) 20 × 9½"	¼" plastic glazing
Spire		
Post	(1) 8'	4 × 4 pressure-treated
Trim	(1) 4'	1 × 2 pressure-treated

Description	No./Size	Material
Molding	(1) 4'	Cap molding, pressure-treated
Balls	(2) 3"-dia.	Wooden sphere, pressure-treated
Roofing		
Sheathing	(4) 4 × 8' sheets	½" exterior-grade plywood roof sheathing
15# building paper	1 roll	
Drip edge	40 linear ft.	Metal drip edge
Shingles	1 square	Asphalt shingles — 250# per sq. min.
Fasteners & Hardware		
16d galvanized common nails	3½ lbs.	
16d common nails	5 lbs.	
10d common nails (for double top plates)	½ lb.	
10d galvanized finish/ casing nails	4 lbs.	
8d galvanized common nails	1 lb.	
8d box nails	2 lbs.	
8d galvanized siding nails	8 lbs.	
1" galvanized roofing nails	3 lbs.	
2" deck screws (for porch decking)	1 lb.	
6d galvanized finish nails	2 lbs.	
3½" galvanized wood screws	24 screws	
1¼" galvanized wood screws	12 screws	
Dowel screws (for spire)	3 screws	Galvanized dowel screws
Lag screws w/washers	2 @ 6"	½" galvanized lag screws
Door hinges w/screws	3	Corrosion-resistant hinges
Door handle/latch	1	
Exterior wood glue		
Clear exterior caulk (for optional window panes)		
Construction adhesive		

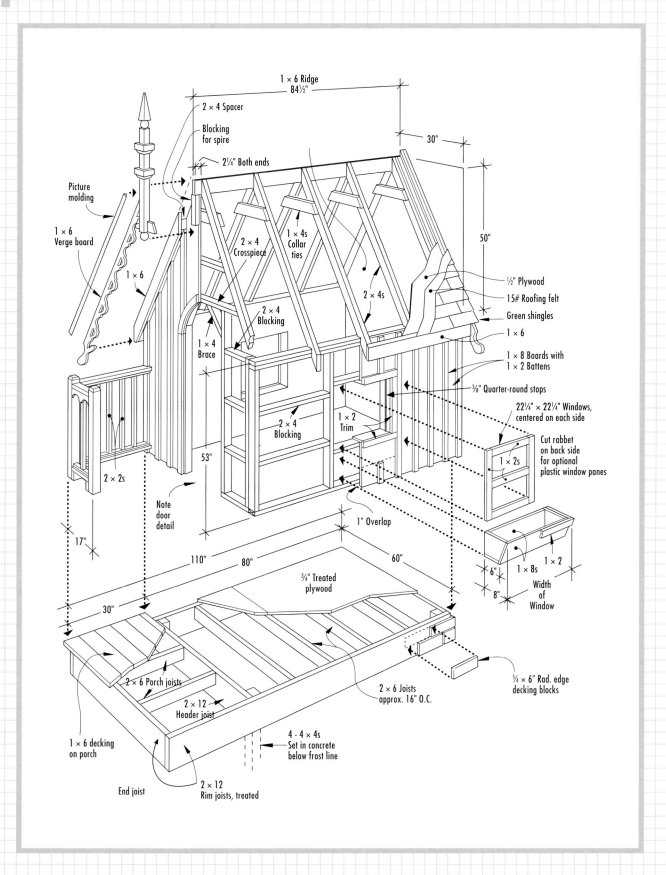

1 × 6 Ridge
84½"

2 × 4 Spacer

Blocking
for spire

2¼" Both ends

30"

Picture
molding

1 × 6
Verge board

1 × 6

50"

½" Plywood

15# Roofing felt

Green shingles

1 × 6

2 × 4
Crosspiece

1 × 4s
Collar
ties

2 × 4s

1 × 8 Boards with
1 × 2 Battens

2 × 4
Blocking

⅜" Quarter-round stops

1 × 4
Brace

22¼" × 22¼" Windows,
centered on each side

Cut rabbet
on back side
for optional
plastic window panes

1 × 2s

1 × 2
Trim

2 × 4
Blocking

53"

2 × 2s

1 × 2s

Note
door
detail

1" Overlap

6"

1 × 8s

1 × 2

Width
of
Window

8"

17"

110"

80"

60"

¾" Treated
plywood

30"

2 × 6 Porch joists

2 × 12
Header joist

2 × 6 Joists
approx. 16" O.C.

⁵⁄₄ × 6" Rad. edge
decking blocks

1 × 6 decking
on porch

End joist

2 × 12
Rim joists, treated

4 - 4 × 4s
Set in concrete
below frost line

Floor Plan

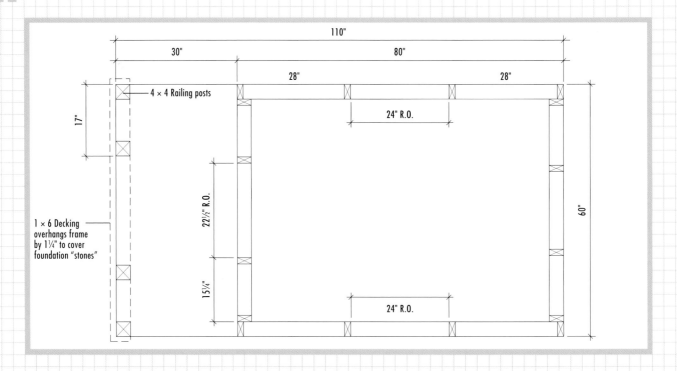

110"

30" | 80"

28" | 28"

4 × 4 Railing posts

17"

24" R.O.

22½" R.O.

1 × 6 Decking overhangs frame by 1¼" to cover foundation "stones"

60"

15¼"

24" R.O.

Verge Board Template

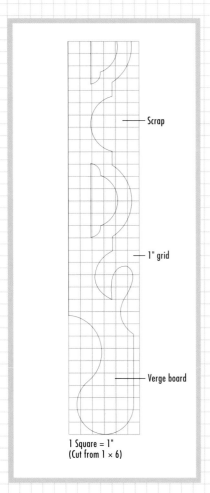

Scrap

1" grid

Verge board

1 Square = 1"
(Cut from 1 × 6)

Deck Railing Detail

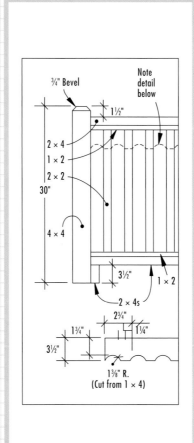

¾" Bevel

Note detail below

1½"

2 × 4

1 × 2

2 × 2

30"

4 × 4

3½"

1 × 2

2 × 4s

2¾"

1¾"

1¼"

3½"

1⅜" R.
(Cut from 1 × 4)

Spire Detail

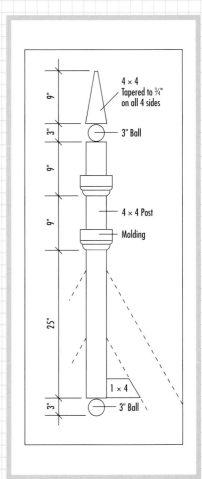

9"

4 × 4
Tapered to ¾"
on all 4 sides

3"

3" Ball

9"

9"

4 × 4 Post

Molding

25"

1 × 4

3"

3" Ball

Door Detail

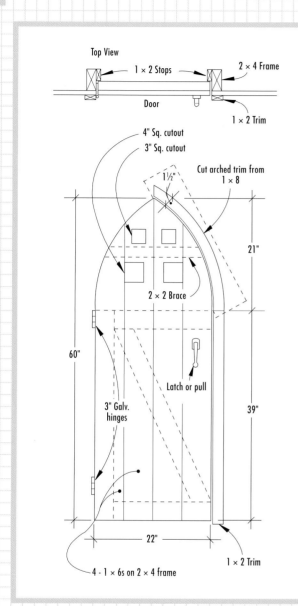

Top View

1 × 2 Stops

2 × 4 Frame

Door

1 × 2 Trim

4" Sq. cutout

3" Sq. cutout

Cut arched trim from 1 × 8

1½"

21"

2 × 2 Brace

Latch or pull

60"

39"

3" Galv. hinges

22"

1 × 2 Trim

4 - 1 × 6s on 2 × 4 frame

Door Arch Template

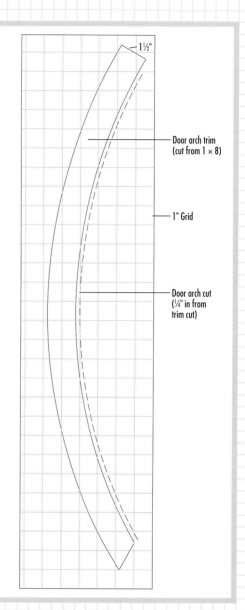

1½"

Door arch trim (cut from 1 × 8)

1" Grid

Door arch cut (¼" in from trim cut)

Board & Batten Detail

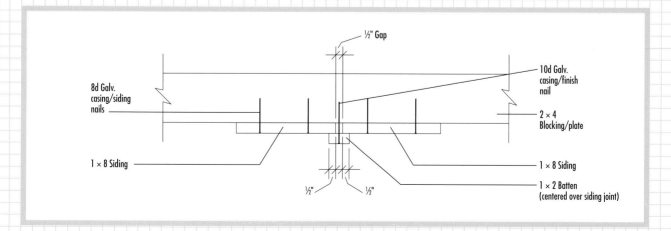

½" Gap

8d Galv. casing/siding nails

10d Galv. casing/finish nail

2 × 4 Blocking/plate

1 × 8 Siding

1 × 8 Siding

1 × 2 Batten (centered over siding joint)

½"   ½"

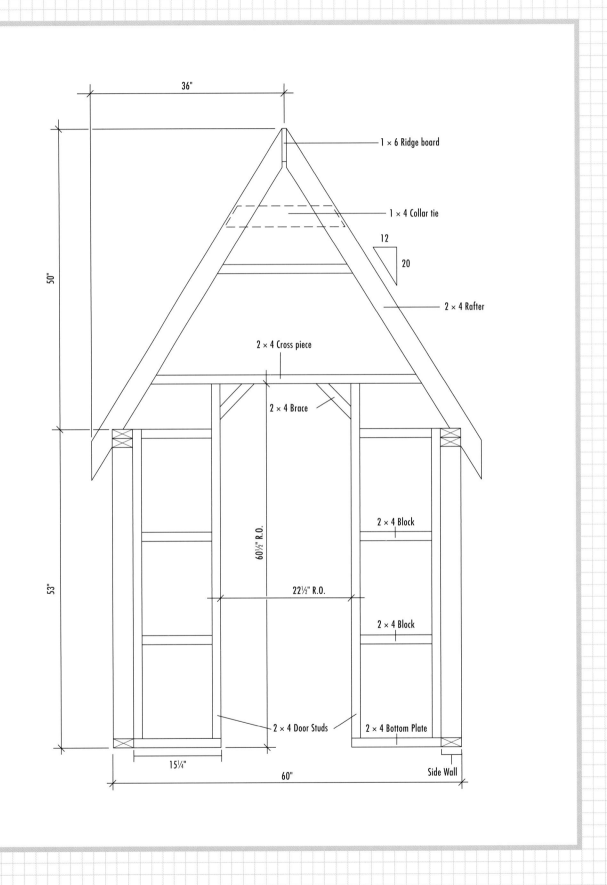

36"

1 × 6 Ridge board

1 × 4 Collar tie

12
20

2 × 4 Rafter

50"

2 × 4 Cross piece

2 × 4 Brace

60½" R.O.

2 × 4 Block

53"

22½" R.O.

2 × 4 Block

2 × 4 Door Studs

2 × 4 Bottom Plate

15¼"

60"

Side Wall

Floor Framing Plan

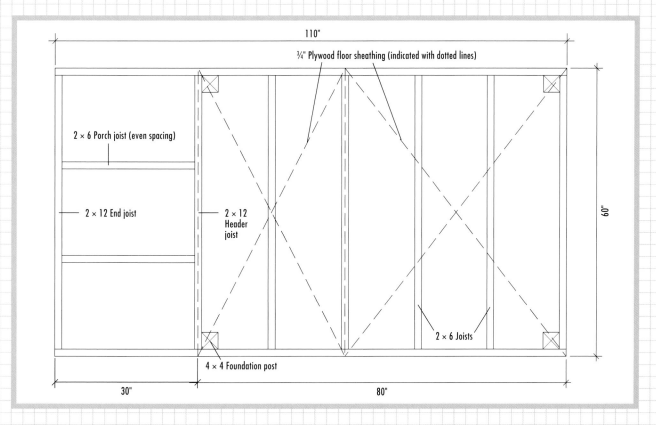

110"

¾" Plywood floor sheathing (indicated with dotted lines)

2 × 6 Porch joist (even spacing)

2 × 12 End joist

2 × 12 Header joist

2 × 6 Joists

60"

4 × 4 Foundation post

30"

80"

Side Framing Plan

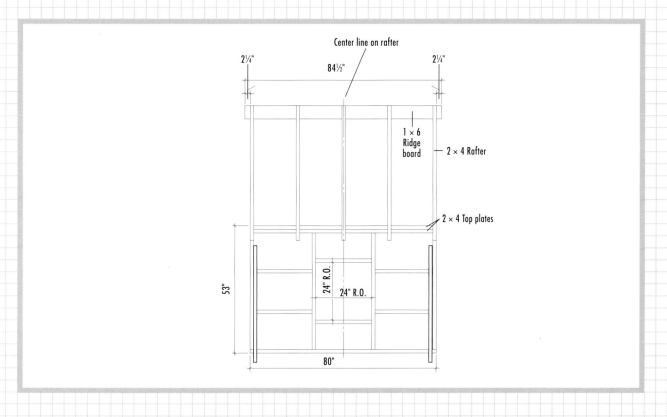

Center line on rafter

2¼"

84½"

2¼"

1 × 6 Ridge board

2 × 4 Rafter

2 × 4 Top plates

53"

24" R.O.

24" R.O.

80"

Rafter Template

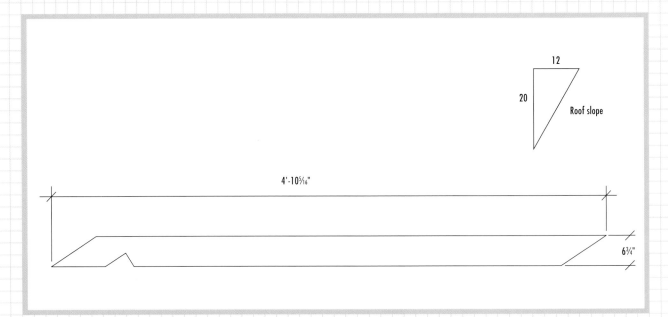

12

20

Roof slope

4'-10⁵⁄₁₆"

6¾"

Window Box Detail

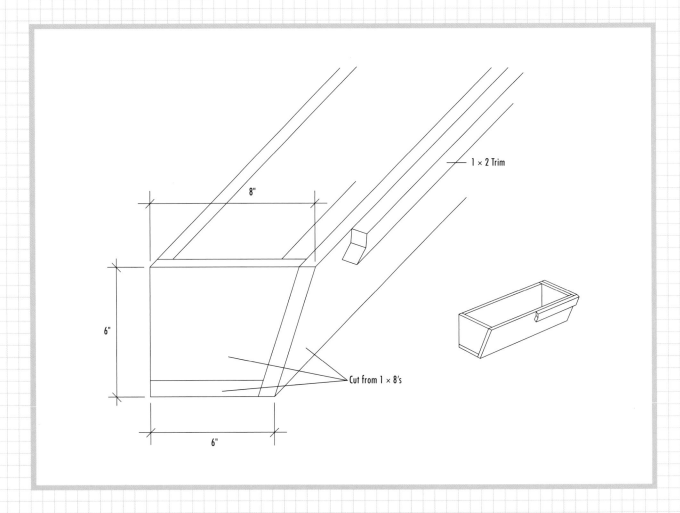

1 × 2 Trim

8"

6"

6"

Cut from 1 × 8's

How to Build the Gothic Playhouse

Set up perpendicular mason's lines and batterboards to plot out the excavation area and the post hole locations, as shown in Floor Framing Plan (page 211). Excavate and grade the construction area, preparing for a 4"-thick gravel base. Dig 12"-dia. holes to a depth below the frost line, plus 4". Add 4" of gravel to each hole. Set the posts in concrete so they extend about 10" above the ground.

After the concrete dries (overnight) add compactable gravel and tamp it down so it is 4" thick and flat. Cut two 2 × 12 rim joists for the floor frame, two 2 × 12 end joists and one header joist. Cut four 2 × 6 joists at 57" and two porch joists at 27¾". Assemble the floor frame with 16d galvanized common nails following Floor Framing Plan (page 211).

Make sure the frame is square and level (prop it up temporarily), and then fasten it to the posts with 16d galvanized common nails.

Cover the interior floor with plywood, starting at the rear end. Trim the second piece so it covers half of the header joist. Install the 1 × 6 porch decking starting at the front edge and leaving a ⅛" gap between boards. Extend the porch decking 1¼" beyond the front and sides of the floor frame.

(continued)

Frame the side walls as shown in the Side Framing (page 211) and Floor Plan (page 208). Each wall has four 2 × 4 studs at 48½", a top and bottom plate at 80", and a 2 × 4 window header and sill at 24". Install the horizontal 2 × 4 blocking, spaced evenly between the plates. Install only one top plate per wall at this time.

Build the rear wall. Raise the side and rear walls, and fasten them to each other and to the floor frame. Add double top plates. Both sidewall top plates should stop flush with the end stud at the front of the wall.

To frame the front wall, cut two treated bottom plates at 15¼", two end studs at 51½" and two door studs at 59". Cut a 2 × 4 crosspiece and two braces, mitering the brace ends at 45°. Cut six 2 × 4 blocks at 12¼". Assemble the wall as shown in the Front Framing (page 210). Raise the front wall and fasten it to the floor and sidewall frames.

Cut one set of 2 × 4 pattern rafters following the Rafter Template (page 212). Test-fit the rafters and make any necessary adjustments. Use one of the pattern rafters to mark and cut the remaining eight rafters. Also cut four 2 × 4 spacers—these should match the rafters but have no birdsmouth cuts.

Cut the ridge board to size and mark the rafter layout following the Side Framing (page 211), and then screw the rafters to the ridge. Cut five 1 × 4 collar ties, mitering the ends at 31°. Fasten the collar ties across each set of rafters so the ends of the ties are flush with the rafter edges. Fasten the 2 × 4 crosspiece above the door to the two end rafters. Install remaining cross-pieces as in the Front Framing (page 210).

Install the 1 × 8 siding boards so they overlap the floor frame by 1" at the bottom and extend to the tops of the side walls, and to the tops of the rafters on the front and rear walls. Gap the boards ½", and fasten them to the framing with pairs of 8d galvanized casing nails or siding nails.

Cut the arched sections of door trim from 1 × 8 lumber, following the Arch Template (page 209). Install the arched pieces and straight 1 × 2 side pieces flush with the inside of the door opening. Wrap the window openings with ripped 1 × 6 boards, and then frame the outsides of the openings with 1 × 2 trim. Install a 1 × 2 batten over each siding joint as shown in Step 10.

Build the 1 × 2 window frames to fit snugly inside the trimmed openings. Assemble the parts with exterior wood glue and galvanized finish nails. If desired, cut a ¼" rabbet in the back side and install plastic windowpanes with silicone caulk. Secure the window frames in the openings with ⅜" quarter-round molding. Construct the window boxes as shown in the Window Box Detail (page 212). Install the boxes below the windows with 1¼" screws.

(continued)

To build the spire, start by drawing a line around a 4 × 4 post, 9" from one end. Draw cutting lines to taper each side down to ¾", as shown in the Spire Detail (page 208). Taper the end with a circular saw or handsaw, and then cut off the point at the 9" mark. Cut the post at 43". Add 1 × 2 trim and cap molding as shown in the detail, mitering the ends at the corners. Drill centered pilot holes into the post, balls, and point, and join the parts with dowel screws.

To cut the verge boards, enlarge the Verge Board Template (page 208) on a photocopier so the squares measure 1". Draw the pattern on a 1 × 6. Cut the board with a jigsaw. Test-fit the board and adjust as needed. Use the cut board as a pattern to mark and cut the remaining verge boards. Install the boards over the front and rear fascia, then add picture molding along the top edges.

Add a 1 × 2 block under the front end of the ridge board. Center the spire at the roof peak, drill pilot holes, and anchor the post with 6" lag screws. Cut and install the 1 × 6 front fascia to run from the spire to the rafter ends, keeping the fascia ½" above the tops of the rafters. Install the rear fascia so it covers the ridge board. Cut and install two 1 × 4 brackets to fit between the spire post and front fascia, as shown in the Spire Detail (page 208).

Cut the 1 × 6 eave fascia to fit between the verge boards, and install it so it will be flush with the top of the roof sheathing. Cut and install the roof sheathing. Add building paper, metal drip edge, and asphalt shingles.

Mark the deck post locations 1¼" in from the ends and front edge of the porch decking, as shown in the Floor Plan. Cut four 4 × 4 railing posts at 30". Bevel the top edges of the posts at 45°, as shown in Deck Railing Detail (page 208). Fasten the posts to the decking and floor frame with 3½" screws. Cut six 2 × 4 treated blocks at 3½". Fasten these to the bottoms of the posts, on the sides that will receive the railings.

Assemble the railing sections following the Deck Railing Detail. Each section has a 2 × 4 top and bottom rail, two 1 × 2 nailers, and 2 × 2 balusters spaced so the edges of the balusters are no more than 4" apart. You can build the sections completely and then fasten them to the posts and front wall, or you can construct them in place starting with the rails. Cut the shaped trim boards from 1 × 4 lumber, using a jigsaw. Notch the rails to fit around the house battens as needed.

Construct the door with 1 × 6 boards fastened to 2 × 4 Z-bracing, as shown in the Door Detail (page 209). Fasten the boards to the bracing with glue and 6d finish nails. Cut the square notches and the top of the door with a jigsaw. Add the 2 × 2 brace as shown. Install the door with two hinges, leaving a ¼" gap all around. Add a knob or latch as desired.

Make the foundation "stones" by cutting (116) 6"-lengths of ¾ × 6 deck boards (the pieces in the top row must be ripped down 1"). Round over the cut edges of all pieces with a router. Attach the top row of stones using construction adhesive and 6d galvanized finish nails. Install the bottom row, starting with a half-piece to create a staggered joint pattern. If desired, finish the playhouse interior with plywood or tongue-and-groove siding.

Log Fort

This is the fort that you wish you'd had when you were a kid. Its three-legged structure and bridge conjure images of pirates, secret hideaways, and buried treasure. The fort is primarily constructed with 6-inch-diameter logs, with some rope accents to give it a rugged outdoor look.

The logs that form the structure for this fort are not readily available at all lumberyards and home improvement centers, so you may have to special-order them. You can substitute 6 × 6 square beams for the round logs and adjust the cuts and notches as necessary. To make the project easier, you can ask a lumberyard or home improvement center to make the angled cuts in the lumber for you or recommend a place that will. On a final note, you'll notice the drawings do not include dimensions for the fascia and beams. You'll need to measure the distances yourself, and for good reason. The chances that all of your corner posts will be perfectly straight and plumb are minimal. If one post is off just a little bit, it will impact the measurements, especially at the top of the structure, so it's best to take the measurements yourself to ensure the boards are cut to the appropriate lengths.

Borrowing materials and techniques from the log-frame construction industry, this fort with play bridge is exceptionally sturdy and built for fun.

Materials List

Description	No./Size	Material
Support System		
Log post	(4) 13'-0"	6"-dia. PT log
Floor Framing		
Log beams	(3) 8'-0"	6"-dia. PT log
Joists, blocking	(6) 6'-0"	2 × 4 PT
Decking	(13) 6'-0"	2 × 6 PT
Spikes	(10) 7"	Rim joist to log
Spikes	(12) 7"	Log to log
Roof Framing		
Rafters	(9) 6'-0"	2 × 6 PT
Hip rafters	(6) 8'-0"	2 × 6 PT
Beams	(6) 8'-0"	2 × 8 PT
Roofing sheathing	(6) 4 × 8'	½" plywood sheathing
Rafter clips	15 with nails	(Simpson H1)
Hold-down straps	3 with nails	(Simpson ST12)
Roof		
Shingles	54 sq. ft.	Asphalt shingles
Roofing felt	54 sq. ft.	15# roofing felt
Metal drip edge	(3) 12'-0"	Galvanized metal
Roofing nails	1.5 lb.	⅞" galvanized
Exterior Finishes		
Fascia trim	(3) 12'-0"	1 × 6 cedar
Fort Railing		
Top/bottom rails	(8) 8'-0"	2 × 6 cedar
Rope railing	160'	¾" dia, nylon rope
Rope anchors	(12) 4"	Lag eye bolt

Description	No./Size	Material
Stair Railing		
Top/bottom rails	(4) 8'-0"	2 × 6 cedar
Rope railing	38'	¾" dia, nylon rope
Carriage bolts	(16) ⅜ × 8"	Galvanized
Rope anchors	(8) 4"	Lag eye bolt
Bridge		
Rope railing	84'	¾"-dia. nylon rope
Decking	(20) 3'-6"	3 × 3 PT (rip-cut from 4 × 4)
Chain	(2) 6'-0"	⁵⁄₁₆"-thick chain
Chain connectors	4	Chain to eye bolt
Eyebolt, washers	(8) ⅜ × 7"	Galvanized
Rope anchors	(4) 4"	Lag eye bolt
Stairs		
Stringer	(2) 8'-0"	2 × 12 PT
Risers	(6) 3'-0"	2 × 12 PT
Top riser	(1) 3"	2 × 8 PT
Riser supports	(12) 8"	12 ga. angle
Top riser supports	(2) 6"	12 ga. angle
Log post	(2) 11'-0"	6"-dia. PT
Log post	(2) 7'-6"	6"-dia. PT
Lag screws, washers	(6) ⅜ × 5"	Galvanized
Miscellaneous		
Box nails	16d, 8d, 6d	Galvanized
Finish nails	16d, 6d	Galvanized
Deck screws	1¼ ×, 2½"	

Tools

Batterboards	Jigsaw
Mason's string	Hammer
Posthole digger or power auger	Square
Pencil and paper	Level
Wood chisel	Protractor
Reciprocating saw	Pliers
Mallet	Ladder
Power miter saw	Drill/driver
Chalk line	Ear and eye protection
Circular saw	Work gloves

Front Elevation

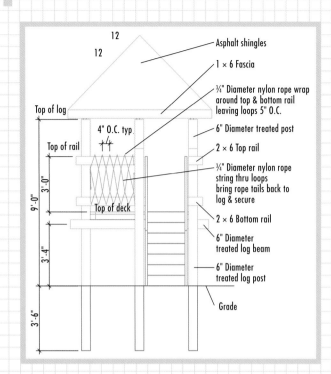

12
12

Top of log

Top of rail

4" O.C. typ.

Top of deck

9'-0"
3'-0"
3'-4"
3'-6"

Asphalt shingles

1 × 6 Fascia

¾" Diameter nylon rope wrap around top & bottom rail leaving loops 5" O.C.

6" Diameter treated post

2 × 6 Top rail

¾" Diameter nylon rope string thru loops bring rope tails back to log & secure

2 × 6 Bottom rail

6" Diameter treated log beam

6" Diameter treated log post

Grade

Left & Right Elevation

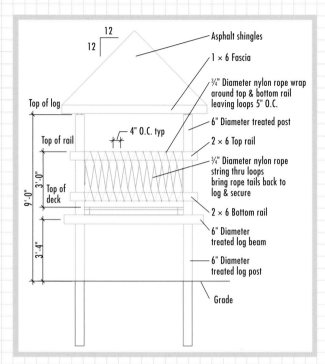

12
12

Top of log

Top of rail

4" O.C. typ

Top of deck

9'-0"
3'-0"
3'-4"

Asphalt shingles

1 × 6 Fascia

¾" Diameter nylon rope wrap around top & bottom rail leaving loops 5" O.C.

6" Diameter treated post

2 × 6 Top rail

¾" Diameter nylon rope string thru loops bring rope tails back to log & secure

2 × 6 Bottom rail

6" Diameter treated log beam

6" Diameter treated log post

Grade

Stair/Bridge Elevation

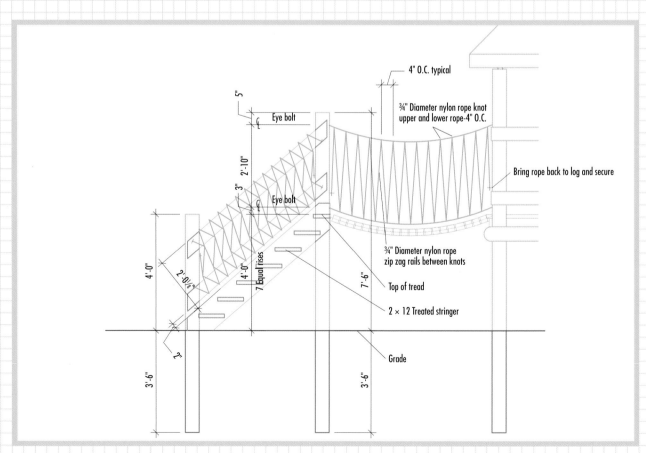

5"

Eye bolt

2'-10"

3"

Eye bolt

4'-0"

2'-0⅛"

4'-0"

7 Equal Rises

2"

3'-6"

4" O.C. typical

¾" Diameter nylon rope knot upper and lower rope-4" O.C.

Bring rope back to log and secure

¾" Diameter nylon rope zip zag rails between knots

Top of tread

2 × 12 Treated stringer

7'-6"

3'-6"

Grade

Floor Framing Plan

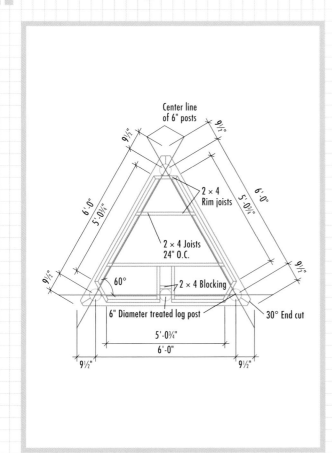

Center line of 6" posts

9½" 9½"

6'-0"
5'-0¾"

6'-0"
5'-0¾"

2 × 4 Rim joists

2 × 4 Joists 24" O.C.

9½"

60°

2 × 4 Blocking

6" Diameter treated log post

30° End cut

9½"

5'-0¾"

6'-0"

9½" 9½"

Railing Detail

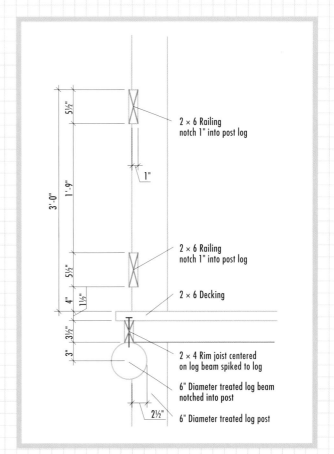

5½"

3'-0"

1'-9"

1"

2 × 6 Railing notch 1" into post log

5½"

2 × 6 Railing notch 1" into post log

4"

1½"

2 × 6 Decking

3½"

3"

2½"

2 × 4 Rim joist centered on log beam spiked to log

6" Diameter treated log beam notched into post

6" Diameter treated log post

Roof Framing Plan

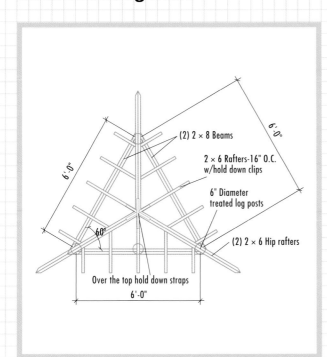

(2) 2 × 8 Beams

2 × 6 Rafters-16" O.C. w/hold down clips

6'-0"

6'-0"

6" Diameter treated log posts

60°

(2) 2 × 6 Hip rafters

Over the top hold down straps

6'-0"

Overhang Detail

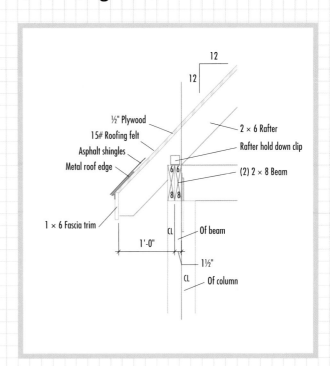

12

12

½" Plywood
15# Roofing felt
Asphalt shingles
Metal roof edge

2 × 6 Rafter
Rafter hold down clip

6 6

8 8

(2) 2 × 8 Beam

1 × 6 Fascia trim

CL   Of beam

1'-0"

1½"

CL   Of column

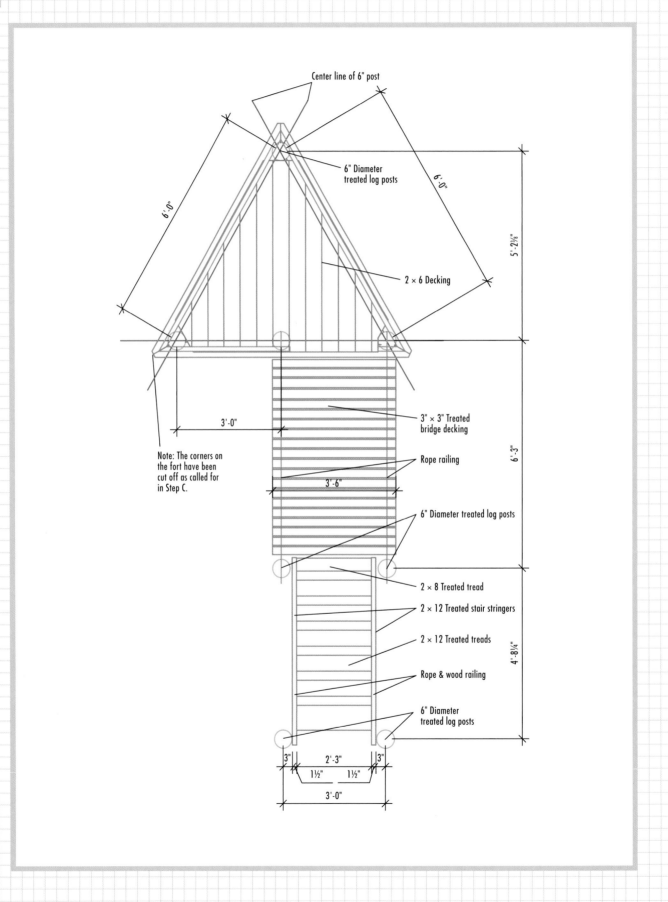

Center line of 6" post

6" Diameter
treated log posts

6'-0"

6'-0"

5'-2⅞"

2 × 6 Decking

3'-0"

Note: The corners on
the fort have been
cut off as called for
in Step C.

3" × 3" Treated
bridge decking

Rope railing

3'-6"

6'-3"

6" Diameter treated log posts

2 × 8 Treated tread

2 × 12 Treated stair stringers

2 × 12 Treated treads

Rope & wood railing

4'-8¼"

6" Diameter
treated log posts

3"   2'-3"   3"
1½"   1½"

3'-0"

How to Build a Log Fort with Bridge

Dig holes for the posts. Use batterboards and mason's line to lay out and mark the post locations, as shown in the diagram on page 220. At the post locations, dig holes 48" deep for the 4 fort posts and 42" deep for the 4 stair posts using a power auger. If you're adding gravel, add 4" to the depth of the holes.

Set the posts in the postholes and brace them so they're level and plumb. Pack the holes with soil (you can also use concrete if you prefer). Measure up and wrap a sheet of paper around each post so the top edge is at the finished post height. Trace the top edge to make a cutting line and cut the posts to height with a reciprocating saw.

Cut half-lap notches in the posts and log beams. Mark the shoulders of the cuts and then use a reciprocating saw to remove waste wood. Finish the cuts with a wide wood chisel and mallet. Make miter cuts for the corners using a large miter saw or a handsaw.

Set the logs into the notched posts, making the lap joints. Test each fit and make adjustments by removing wood until all the log ends fit together cleanly. Drive two 7" spikes through the log into the post at each end. Once the joints are secure, cut 3" off the ends of the logs at each corner to create a blunt edge.

Frame in the deck. Cut two rim joists to length with a 60° angle on each end and cut two with a 30° angle on one end and a square cut on the other end. Fasten the joists on top of the logs using 7" spikes driven through pilot holes. Cut the short end pieces to fit between the longer rim joists and nail them to the posts to close the deck framing.

(continued)

Install the deck boards. Cut a 2 × 6 deck board and center it on the rim joists between the back post and front center post. Fasten it to the joists with 2½" deck screws. Install the remaining deck boards, maintaining a ⅛" gap. Snap a chalk line over the ends of the deck boards, flush with the outside edges of the rim joists and trim with a circular saw. Use a jigsaw to cut places the circular saw can't reach.

Install the railing. Cut notches in the posts for the top and bottom deck rails. Place 2 × 6 rails so they fit into the notches and mark the cutting angles at the ends where the rails meet. Make the miter cuts according to your marks. Install the front rails, fitting the angled ends together with the side rails and keeping the square ends flush with the edges of posts, and then install the second row of railing.

Install the roof beams. Measure the distance between the centers of the three corner posts. Cut a 2 × 8 beam with a 30° angle on each end so the long end of the angles is at the center of the posts. Toenail the beams to the posts with 16d galvanized common nails. Measure the distances between the outside edges of the beams and cut a beam to fit each spot. Facenail the beams together using 16d nails driven at a slight angle and toenail the beams to the posts.

Rafter hold-down straps

Birdsmouth

Frame the roof. Cut the hip rafters and rafters and then facenail the hip rafters together in pairs. Mark the hip rafters for the rafter locations 16" on center. Nail the hip rafters in place. Mark each beam at the centerpoint for a 2 × 6 rafter and then toenail the rafters in place. Reinforce the connections by installing rafter hold-down clips.

10

Sheathing

Felt paper

Fascia

Drip edge

Install the fascia and sheathing. Cut 1 × 6 fascia trim boards to fit around the perimeter of the roof, mitering the corners at 30°. Nail the fascia to the rafter ends. Cut ½" plywood sheathing to make the roof deck and nail the panels in place. Install metal drip edge molding (drip edge) and then staple 15# building paper over the sheathing and drip edge. Shingle the roof.

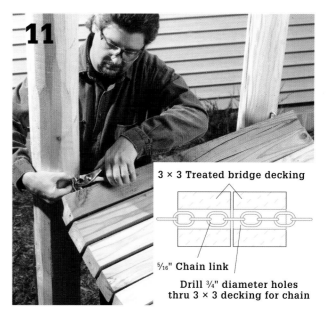

11

3 × 3 Treated bridge decking

⁵⁄₁₆" Chain link

Drill ¾" diameter holes thru 3 × 3 decking for chain

Build the bridge. The bridge is suspended by chains that are threaded through holes in the bridge decking and anchored to ⅜ × 7" eyebolts in the posts at the bridge ends. Use ⁵⁄₁₆" chain inserted through ¾" guide holes. Cut twenty 3 × 3 bridge decking boards at 42" (you can rip-cut deck boards from 4 × 4 post stock). Drill two ¾" holes through each board, 3" from the outside edges.

12

Build the stairs. Use a pair of 2 × 12 stringers to support the treads. Make the top tread from a 2 × 8, and the rest from 2 × 12. Lay out the stair tread locations on the stringers (see the diagram, page 222) and attach the treads with metal stair angle hardware secured to the stringers with deck screws.

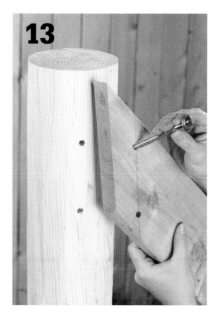

13

Install rails. Cut the stair rails to length with a plumb cut at each end (approximately 50°, but check the actual parts with a level and protractor) and attach them to the posts with ⅜ × 5" lag screws.

14

Install the rope rails. Attach a ⅜ × 7" eyebolt with washer at each bolt location (see the diagram, page 222). Insert ¾" nylon rope through each set of eye bolts on both sides of the bridge. Wrap rope around the rails 4" on center, then weave a third rope through the rope on the rails to fill in the area between the rails as shown. Ropes should be tied between rails on the stairs, bridge and fort deck.

Clubhouse

A clubhouse is a proven favorite for children of all ages. This clubhouse features several fun components to keep kids engaged, including a sandbox, trap-door with rope, open deck, and enclosed play structure.

The floor of the clubhouse sits eight feet off the ground. The elevated structure adds to the excitement of play, especially when kids can escape by lifting the trap-door and sliding down the rope. The clubhouse features openings on all four sides as well as openings on the gable ends to allow for sunlight and air circulation. The openings are at safe heights to prevent injuries.

While the clubhouse is not fully watertight, it does have a shingled roof to protect against wind and rain. The deck gives children an open air area to enjoy while playing. The sandbox underneath the deck maximizes space and offers yet another way for kids to have fun.

The construction of the clubhouse is fairly straightforward, with everything built on six 4 × 4 posts. It's sure to be the focus of your backyard and provide years of fun for your family.

This split-level funhouse features distinct play areas and just the right amount of kids-only clubhouse space.

Materials List

Description	No./Size	Material
Support System		
Posts	(4) 12'-0"	4 × 4 Pressure-treated pine
Posts	(2) 9'-0"	4 × 4 Pressure-treated pine
Cross bridging	(2) 8'-0"	2 × 4 Pressure-treated pine
Baseboard	(3) 6'-0"	2 × 12 Pressure-treated pine
Baseboard	(2) 8'-0"	2 × 12 Pressure-treated pine
Floor Framing		
Rim joists	(8) 6'-0"	2 × 6 Pressure-treated pine
Rim joists	(4) 8'-0"	2 × 6 Pressure-treated pine
Joists	(2) 8'-0"	2 × 6 Pressure-treated pine
Trapdoor header	(1) 4'-0"	2 × 6 Pressure-treated pine
Trapdoor stop	(1) 8'-0"	2 × 4 Pressure-treated pine
Trapdoor nailer	(1) 8'-0"	2 × 4 Pressure-treated pine
Decking	(17) 6'-0"	2 × 6 Pressure-treated pine
Joist hangers	8 w/nails	(Simpson U26)
Rim joist hangers	16 w/nails	(Simpson HUC26 — 2)
Wall Framing		
Purlins	(3) 10'-0"	2 × 4
Door jambs	(3) 8'-0"	2 × 4
Top plates	(4) 10'-0"	2 × 4
Studs	(2) 8'-0"	2 × 4
Gable studs	(1) 4'-0"	2 × 4
Roof Framing		
Rafters	(4) 8'-0"	2 × 6
Ridge	(1) 6'-0"	2 × 8
Gable stud	(1) 6'-0"	2 × 4
Rope supports	(1) 4'-0"	2 × 6
Roof sheathing	(2) 4 × 8'	½" plywood
Hold-down clips	8 w/nails	(Simpson H3)
Sandbox		
Frame	(3) 8'-0"	2 × 4 Pressure-treated pine
Side plates, braces	(1) 8'-0"	2 × 6 Pressure-treated pine
Stops/mid support	(4) 8'-0"	2 × 2 Pressure-treated pine
Screen	(1) 4' × 5'	Poultry netting
Hinge	2 w/screws	3 × 3" exterior butt
Handle	1 w/screws	6" door pull

Description	No./Size	Material
Latch	2 w/screws	Gate latch
Exterior Finishes		
Siding	(18) 10'-0"	1 × 8 V-joint cedar
Fascia	(2) 6'-0"	1 × 6 cedar
Roof		
Shingles	64 sq. ft.	Asphalt 3-tab
Roofing felt	64 sq. ft.	15# roofing felt
Metal drip edge	(4) 8'-0"	Galv. metal
Roofing nails	½ lb.	⅞" galvanized
Stairs		
Stringer	(2) 10'-0"	2 × 10 Pressure-treated pine
Treads	(3) 8'-0"	2 × 6 Pressure-treated pine
Tread clips	(24) 4"	16-ga. angle iron
Angle brackets	2	
Lag screws, washers	(156) ¼" × 1¼"	Galvanized
Stair footing	(1) 4'-0"	2 × 12 Pressure-treated pine
Deck and Stair Railing		
Top rail	(3) 10'-0"	2 × 6 cedar
Top rail	(1) 6'-0"	2 × 6 cedar
Balusters	(47) 4'-0"	2 × 2 cedar
Railing posts	(3) 4'-0"	4 × 4 cedar
Carriage bolts	(6) ⅜" × 5"	Galvanized
Nailer	(1) 6'-0"	2 × 2 Pressure-treated pine
Deck fascia	(1) 6'-0"	2 × 8 cedar
Deck fascia	(2) 8'-0"	2 × 8 cedar
Miscellaneous		
Trap door hinge	(1) 18"	2" butt hinge
Fasteners (Galvanized)		
Common nails	4 lbs. 16d	
Common nails	2 lbs. 10d	
Box nails	1 lb. 6d	
Trim/finish nails	½ lb. 6d	
Coated nails	½ lb. 4d	
Deck screws	(25) 2½"	
Sand		
Rope		

Front Elevation

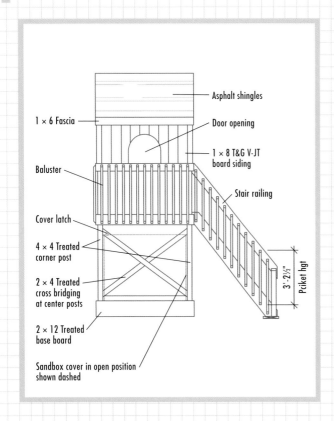

1 × 6 Fascia

Baluster

Cover latch

4 × 4 Treated corner post

2 × 4 Treated cross bridging at center posts

2 × 12 Treated base board

Sandbox cover in open position shown dashed

Asphalt shingles

Door opening

1 × 8 T&G V-JT board siding

Stair railing

3'-2½" Pciket hgt

Rear Elevation

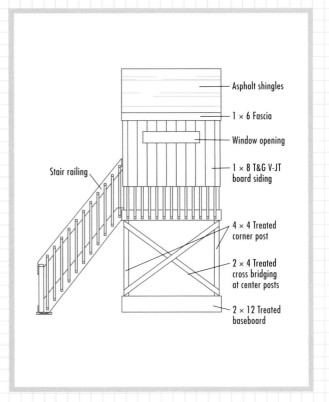

Stair railing

Asphalt shingles

1 × 6 Fascia

Window opening

1 × 8 T&G V-JT board siding

4 × 4 Treated corner post

2 × 4 Treated cross bridging at center posts

2 × 12 Treated baseboard

Building Section

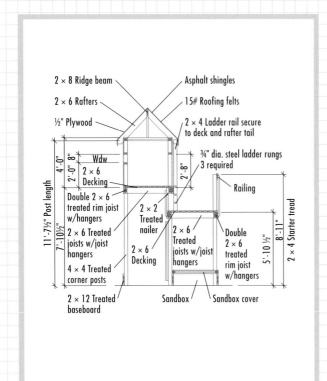

2 × 8 Ridge beam

2 × 6 Rafters

½" Plywood

Asphalt shingles

15# Roofing felts

2 × 4 Ladder rail secure to deck and rafter tail

¾" dia. steel ladder rungs 3 required

4'-0"   Wdw   8"
2'-0"   2 × 6
Decking

Double 2 × 6 treated rim joist w/hangers

2 × 6 Treated joists w/joist hangers

4 × 4 Treated corner posts

2 × 12 Treated baseboard

11'-7½" Post length   7'-10½"

2 × 2 Treated nailer

2 × 6 Decking

2 × 6 Treated joists w/joist hangers

Sandbox

2'-8"

Railing

Double 2 × 6 treated rim joist w/hangers

5'-10½"   8'-1"   2 × 4 Starter tread

Sandbox cover

Right Elevation

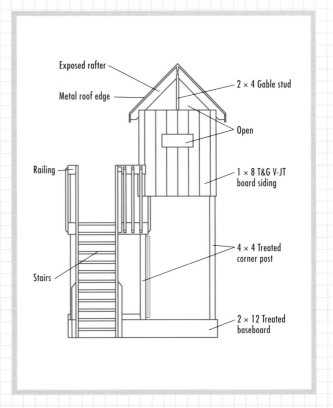

Exposed rafter

Metal roof edge

Railing

Stairs

2 × 4 Gable stud

Open

1 × 8 T&G V-JT board siding

4 × 4 Treated corner post

2 × 12 Treated baseboard

Base Framing

Floor Framing Clubhouse

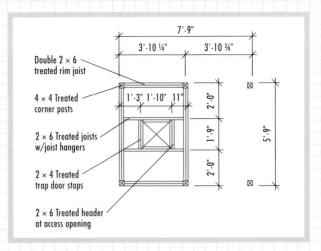

Front/Rear/Right Side/Left Side Framing

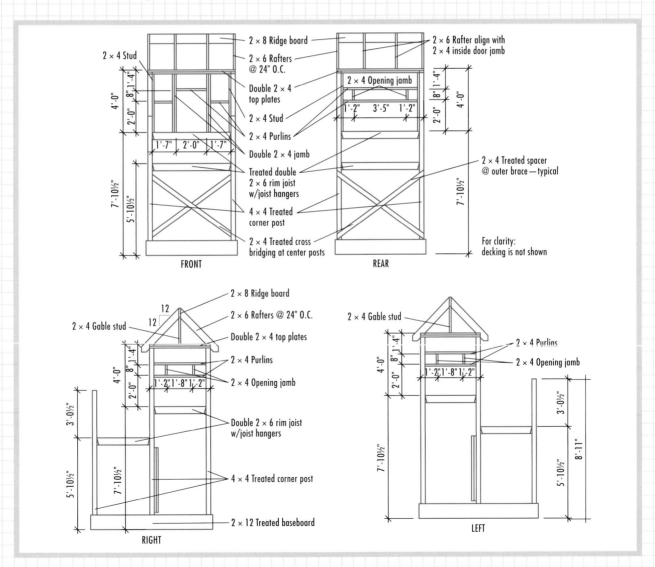

Clubhouse Roof Framing

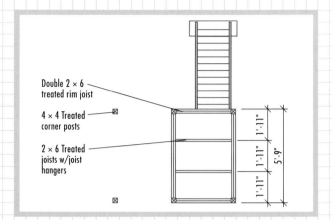

5½"   4'-0"   5½"

Overhang

5'-9"

2 × 6 rafter

2 × 6 Rafter align with 2× inside door jamb

2 × 4 Ladder stringer

2 × 6 Rafter

2 × 8 Ridge

Deck Floor Framing

Double 2 × 6 treated rim joist

4 × 4 Treated corner posts

2 × 6 Treated joists w/joist hangers

1'-11"   1'-11"   1'-11"   5'-9"

Floor Plan

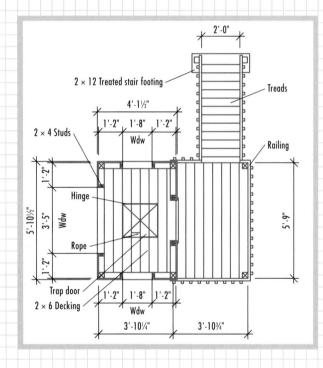

2'-0"

2 × 12 Treated stair footing

Treads

4'-1½"

1'-2"   1'-8"   1'-2"

Wdw

2 × 4 Studs

Railing

1'-2"

5'-10½"   3'-5"

Wdw

Hinge

Rope

5'-9"

1'-2"

Trap door

2 × 6 Decking

1'-2"   1'-8"   1'-2"

Wdw

3'-10¼"   3'-10¾"

Stair Section

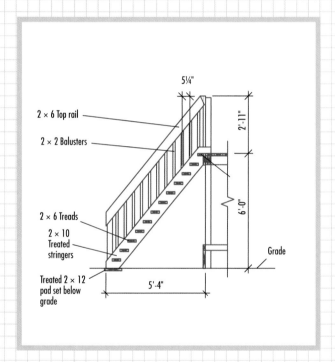

5¼"

2 × 6 Top rail

2 × 2 Balusters

2'-11"

2 × 6 Treads

2 × 10 Treated stringers

6'-0"

Treated 2 × 12 pad set below grade

Grade

5'-4"

Sandbox Plan

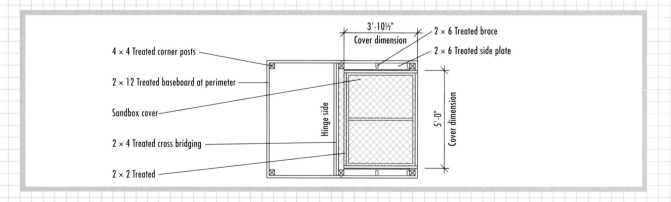

4 × 4 Treated corner posts

2 × 12 Treated baseboard at perimeter

Sandbox cover

2 × 4 Treated cross bridging

2 × 2 Treated

3'-10½"

Cover dimension

2 × 6 Treated brace

2 × 6 Treated side plate

Hinge side

5'-0"

Cover dimension

How to Build a Clubhouse

Assemble the base. Fasten the 4 baseboards using 16d nails and then install the middle baseboard. Set a post in the corner, plumb it and fasten it with 16d nails. Install posts in all 4 corners. Install 2 × 4 cross bridging on 1 side (see Base Framing Plan, page 229). Add two center posts.

Frame the floor. Install a double joist hanger on the face of each post. Face-nail 2 rim joists together and then fasten a pair in each bracket with 10d nails. Attach hangers and then install the inner rim joists (single). Frame the trap door opening.

Install the floor decking. Cut the first piece of decking to length and then cut 3½ × 3½" notches on both ends to fit around the posts using a jigsaw. Attach the decking with 2½" deck screws. Position the remaining boards so they are flush with the rim joists and attach them with deck screws. As the trapdoor access opening is covered, trim each board flush with the header and joists using a jigsaw.

Build and install the trapdoor. Place the door boards perpendicular to the 2 × 4 trapdoor nailers, overhanging 1½" on both ends and 2½" on both sides and attach with deck screws. Drill a 1"-dia. rope access hole 3" from the edge. Face-nail 2 × 4 trapdoor stops around the access opening. Place the door in the access opening and fasten with hinges.

(continued)

Frame the walls. Facenail the corner studs against the front and rear clubhouse posts using 16d nails. Fasten all top plates, doubling them as shown in the diagram on page 229. Install the door jamb, making sure it is level and plumb. Add 2 × 4 purlins between the jambs to function as nailers.

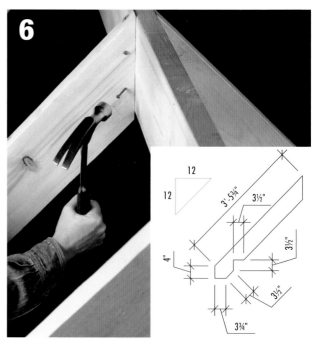

Frame the roof. Cut two 2 × 6 pattern rafters following the rafter illustration (inset). Use a jigsaw to cut the birdsmouth. Place the rafters on the top plates and test-fit them using a 2 × 8 spacer block. Cut the remaining six rafters. Nail the rafters to the top plates and the ridge board at the proper locations. Install clips to reinforce the connection between the rafters and the top plates.

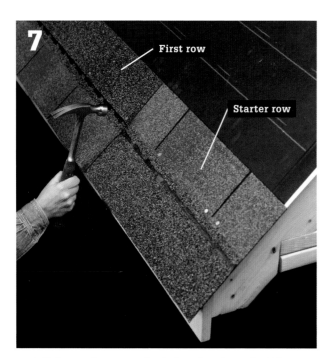

Install the roof. Fasten a fascia board to the ends of the rafters on each side. Nail or screw ½" plywood sheathing onto the rafters. Place metal roof edge (drip edge) along the sides and bottom of the sheathing. Cover the roof with 15# felt paper and staple it to the sheathing. Install shingles.

Install the siding. Starting at a corner, fasten the siding to the framing using 4d coated common nails. Drive two nails at the top and bottom of the board and at the purlins. On the front and rear sides of the clubhouse, cut notches in the top of the boards using a jigsaw to fit around the rafters. As the siding is installed, cut the window openings.

Build the landing deck. Nail joist hangers on the inside faces of the posts in the landing area and then install double joists in the hangers. Attach single joists between the double joists to support the deck boards. Install the deck boards. Fasten deck fascia boards to the deck using 2½" deck screws.

Build the stairs. Lay out the stair stringers on 2 × 10 pressure-treated lumber. Cut the stringer ends and then cut the notches in the ends of the stringers to fit over the deck. Fasten tread clips and attach angle brackets to the stringers. Center the stair footing under the stringers and fasten it using 2½" deck screws. Fasten the stringers to the deck and then install the treads.

Install the deck railing. Attach the deck rail posts on top of the stair footing, using ⅜ × 5" carriage bolts. Install a deck rail across the front corner posts so the ends are flush with the outside edges of the posts. Install rails along the left and right sides of the deck, securing them with deck screws.

Install the balusters. Drill two ⅛" pilot holes near the bottom end of each baluster (picket), spaced about 4" apart. Drill two pilot holes near the top of the balusters, spaced 1½" apart. For the rear balusters, drill the top holes ¾" apart. Cut a 2 × 6 spacer at 3¾". Install the balusters using the spacer to ensure uniform gaps.

(continued)

Install stair railing. Install a baluster at the top end of each stair stringer. Mark and cut the ends of the rails to be flush with the posts and then attach the rails with deck screws. Install balusters along the stairs, using the 3¾" spacer as a guide.

Install side plates for the sandbox. Cut 45°-angled braces and attach them to the posts and bases using deck screws. Fasten the side plates to the baseboards and the braces using wood screws.

Build the sandbox cover frame and then fasten poultry netting to the edges of the frame. Attach it with butt hinges, then raise the cover and mark the locations for the latches on the cross brace. Install a latch on each end of the door.

Attach the rope. Center the two 20" rope supports on the ridge board over the trapdoor opening and attach them. Using a plumb bob hung from the ridge board, mark the location on the ridge directly above the rope opening in the trapdoor. Drill a 1" hole through the supports and ridge board and then insert the rope through the hole and securely tie the end.

Conversions Charts

Converting Measurements

To Convert:	To:	Multiply by:
Inches	Millimeters	25.4
Inches	Centimeters	2.54
Feet	Meters	0.305
Yards	Meters	0.914
Square inches	Square centimeters	6.45
Square feet	Square meters	0.093
Square yards	Square meters	0.836
Cubic inches	Cubic centimeters	16.4
Cubic feet	Cubic meters	0.0283
Cubic yards	Cubic meters	0.765
Pounds	Kilograms	0.454

To Convert:	To:	Multiply by:
Millimeters	Inches	0.039
Centimeters	Inches	0.394
Meters	Feet	3.28
Meters	Yards	1.09
Square centimeters	Square inches	0.155
Square meters	Square feet	10.8
Square meters	Square yards	1.2
Cubic centimeters	Cubic inches	0.061
Cubic meters	Cubic feet	35.3
Cubic meters	Cubic yards	1.31
Kilograms	Pounds	2.2

Lumber Dimensions

Nominal - U.S.	Actual - U.S. (in inches)	Metric
1 × 2	¾ × 1½	19 × 38 mm
1 × 3	¾ × 2½	19 × 64 mm
1 × 4	¾ × 3½	19 × 89 mm
1 × 5	¾ × 4½	19 × 114 mm
1 × 6	¾ × 5½	19 × 140 mm
1 × 7	¾ × 6¼	19 × 159 mm
1 × 8	¾ × 7¼	19 × 184 mm
1 × 10	¾ × 9¼	19 × 235 mm
1 × 12	¾ × 11¼	19 × 286 mm
2 × 2	1½ × 1½	38 × 38 mm

Nominal - U.S.	Actual - U.S. (in inches)	Metric
2 × 3	1½ × 2½	38 × 64 mm
2 × 4	1½ × 3½	38 × 89 mm
2 × 6	1½ × 5½	38 × 140 mm
2 × 8	1½ × 7¼	38 × 184 mm
2 × 10	1½ × 9¼	38 × 235 mm
2 × 12	1½ × 11¼	38 × 286 mm
4 × 4	3½ × 3½	89 × 89 mm
4 × 6	3½ × 5½	89 × 140 mm
6 × 6	5½ × 5½	140 × 140 mm
8 × 8	7¼ × 7¼	184 × 184 mm

Metric Plywood

Standard Sheathing Grade	Sanded Grade
7.5 mm (5⁄16")	6 mm (4⁄17")
9.5 mm (3⁄8")	8 mm (5⁄16")
12.5 mm (½")	11 mm (7⁄16")
15.5 mm (5⁄8")	14 mm (9⁄16")
18.5 mm (¾")	17 mm (2⁄3")
20.5 mm (13⁄16")	19 mm (¾")
22.5 mm (7⁄8")	21 mm (13⁄16")
25.5 mm (1")	24 mm (15⁄16")

Counterbore, Shank & Pilot Hole Diameters

Screw Size	Counterbore Diameter for Screw Head	Clearance Hole for Screw Shank	Pilot Hole Diameter	
			Hard Wood	Soft Wood
#1	.146 (9⁄64)	5⁄64	3⁄64	1⁄32
#2	¼	3⁄32	3⁄64	1⁄32
#3	¼	7⁄64	1⁄16	3⁄64
#4	¼	1⁄8	1⁄16	3⁄64
#5	¼	1⁄8	5⁄64	1⁄16
#6	5⁄16	9⁄64	3⁄32	5⁄64
#7	5⁄16	5⁄32	3⁄32	5⁄64
#8	3⁄8	11⁄64	1⁄8	3⁄32
#9	3⁄8	11⁄64	1⁄8	3⁄32
#10	3⁄8	3⁄16	1⁄8	7⁄64
#11	½	3⁄16	5⁄32	9⁄64
#12	½	7⁄32	9⁄64	1⁄8

Resources

Black & Decker
Portable power tools and more
www.blackanddecker.com

Red Wing Shoes Co,
Work shoes and boots shown
    throughout book
800-733-9464
www.redwingshoes.com

PLAYGROUND SAFETY
**National Program for Playground
    Safety**
(800) 554-PLAY
www.uni.edu/playground

**Consumer Product Safety
    Commission**
(800) 638-2772
www.cpsc.gov
Outdoor Home Playground Safety
    Handbook by the Consumer Product
    Safety Commission is available at
    www.cpsc.gov/CPSCPUB/PUBS/324.pdf

PLAYGROUNDS & PLAYGROUND EQUIPMENT
Playstar
(888) 752-9782
www.playstarinc.com

Swingworks (p.59)
(877) 447-9464
www.swingworks.com

Detailed Play Systems
(800) 398-7565
www.detailedplay.com

Swingsetaccessories.com
(616) 437-5179
www.swingsetaccessories.com

CedarWorks
(800) 462-3327
www.cedarworks.com

Rubberscapes
(888) 665-1119
www.rubberscapes.net

Surface America
(800) 999-0555
www.surfaceamerica.com

SEESAWS
Nater Tater's Teeter Totters
(765) 714-5423
www.ntteetertotters.com

Swingsets and More.com
(800) 632-6902
www.swingsetsandmore.com

CLIMBING NETS
Custom Cargo Nets.com
(877) 206-8967
www.customcargonets.com

TREEHOUSE INFORMATION & HARDWARE
Treehouses.com
(541) 592-2208
www.treehouses.com/treehouse/
    construction

ZIP LINES
Outdoor Fun Store Co.
(877) 386-1700
www.outdoorfunstore.com/zipline

Zip Line Gear
(888) 476-3701
www.ziplinegear.com

ICE RINKS
Nice Rink
(888) 642-3746
www.nicerink.com

Mybackyardicerink.com
(888) 927-3423
www.mybackyardicerink.com

SKATEBOARD RAMPS
Ramp Plans Dot Org
www.rampplans.org

Rick Dahlen (p.98)
www.rickdahlen.com/pipepix/halfpipe

BASKETBALL
Goalrilla
(888) 872-4625
www.goalrilla.com

Spalding
(800) 772-5346
www.spalding.com

BOCCE
Boccemon.com
(360) 224-2909
www.boccemon.com

United States Bocce Federation
(630) 257-2854
www.bocce.com

BATTING CAGES
Batting Cages, Inc.
(800) 463-6865
www.battingcagesinc.com

Action Sports Company
(800) 580-0307
www.actionsportscompany.com

GOLF NET
Criterion Athletic
(800) 463-6865
www.criterionathletic.com

Action Sports Company
(800) 580-0307
www.actionsportscompany.com

HORSESHOES
**National Horseshoe Pitchers
    Association of America**
www.horseshoepitching.com

SPORTS COURT
Sport Court North (p.114)
(888) 925-4667
www.sportcourtmn.com

Sport Court
(800) 421-8112
www.sportcourt.com

TETHERBALL
Total Tetherball
www.toteth.com

PICKLEBALL
Pickle-ball, Inc.
(800) 377-9915
www.pickleball.com

USA Pickleball Association
www.usapa.org

SPORTS BOUNDARY LINES
Stackhouse Athletic Equipment
(800) 285-3604
www.stackhouseathletic.com

PUTTING GREEN
Backyard Golf
(949) 887-2302
www.backyardgolf.us

Synthetic Turf International
(877) 784-8873
www.synthetic-turf.com

Residential Putting Green Magazine
www.residential-putting-green-magazine.
   com

BEANBAG TOSS
American Cornhole Association
www.playcornhole.org

SWIMMING POOLS
Splash SuperPools
(501) 945-4999
www.splashpools.com

EZ Pool Products
(714) 979-7921
www.reallyezpools.com

SWIM SPA
Endless Pools
(800) 732-8660
www.endlesspools.com

OUTDOOR SOUND
Bose
(800) 999-2673
www.bose.com

Klipsch
(800) 554-7724
www.klipsch.com

SAUNAS
Northern Lights Cedar Tubs, Inc.
(800) 759-8990
www.cedarbarrelsaunas.com

Finlandia Sauna
(800) 354-3342
www.finlandiasauna.com

Saunas.com
(800) 906-2242
www.saunas.com

OUTDOOR CAMERAS
Bushnell
(866) 255-8406
www.shopbushnell.com

Wingscapes
(888) 811-9464
www.wingscapes.com

Birdhouse Spy Cam
(800) 807-1030
www.birdhousespycam.com

BACKYARD THEATRE
Backyard Theatre.com
www.backyardtheater.com

Open Air Cinema
(866) 802-8202
www.openaircinema.us

Carl's Place
(608) 352-0002
www.carlofet.com

Dazian Fabrics
(877) 232-9426
www.dazian.com

PATIO HEATERS
Patio Heater Store.com
(866) 579-5182
www.patioheaterstore.com

Solaira
(905) 568-7655 ext. 21
www.solairaheaters.com

Photography Credits

Index